SHORT BIKE RIDES™
IN HAWAII

Short Bike Rides™ Series

Short Bike Rides™ in Hawaii

By

William L. Walters

Old Saybrook, Connecticut

To my father,
Jess H. Walters

Copyright © 1998 by William L. Walters

Short Bike Rides is a trademark of The Globe Pequot Press
Cover photograph: Images © 1996 PhotoDisc, Inc.
Text design: Mary Ballachino
Photos by William L. Walters

Library of Congress Cataloging-in-Publication Data

Walters, William L.
      Short bike rides in Hawaii / by William L. Walters.
         p. cm.—(Short bike rides series)
      ISBN 0-7627-0116-1
      1. Bicycle touring—Hawaii—Guidebooks. 2. Hawaii—Guidebooks.
I. Title.   II. Series
GV1045.5.H3W35   1997
919.6904'41—dc21   97-30178
                                        CIP

♻ This book is printed on recycled paper.
Manufactured in the United States of America
First Edition/First Printing

Contents

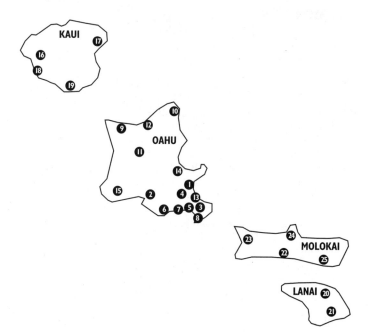

KAUI

17
16
18
19

OAHU

10
12
9
11
14
1
4
13
15
2
6 7 5 3
8

MOLOKAI

23
24
22
25

LANAI
20
21

Hawaii

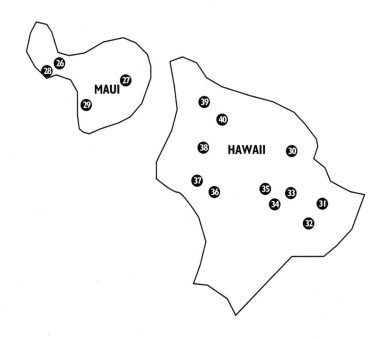

Help Us Keep This Guide Up to Date

Every effort has been made by the author and editors to make this guide as accurate and useful as possible. However, many things can change after a guide is published—establishments close, phone numbers change, trails are rerouted, facilities come under new management, etc.

We would love to hear from you concerning your experiences with this guide and how you feel it could be made better and be kept up to date. While we may not be able to respond to all comments and suggestions, we'll take them to heart and we'll also make certain to share them with the author. Please send your comments and suggestions to the following address:

The Globe Pequot Press
Reader Response/Editorial Department
P.O. Box 833
Old Saybrook, CT 06475

Or you may e-mail us at:

editorial@globe-pequot.com

Thanks for your input, and happy travels!

Introduction

The ritual of getting your bike ready for a ride is the same no matter where you are. But in Hawaii—even in the early-morning darkness as you pump up the tires, lube the chain, and strap on your helmet—you sense you are somewhere special. The sweet smell of flowering trees, soft breezes from the northeast, and the faint aroma of sea salt leave no doubt that you are in the Hawaiian Islands.

Literally built from the ground up, these islands were created by volcanoes that erupted from hot spots on the ocean floor and rose to thousands of feet above the sea. Life began slowly, first in the form of lichens, then ferns and trees. Brought to Hawaii by chance on the Pacific winds, a few select insects, birds, and other animals made the islands home.

The names of the islands as we know them today reverberate in the language of the people who discovered them. The first Hawaiians, with intimate knowledge of ocean and stars, navigated to and from the islands without compass or sextant. The Hawaiian language and culture, later overwhelmed by the influences of Western society, are emerging again as people learn to value them for being as unique as the islands themselves.

Visitors to Hawaii will find every terrain and climate imaginable. You can ride near sandy beaches, through tropical jungles, and over barren lava fields. You can glide over flat roads and rolling hills, or you can take on a spectacular climb from sea level to the 10,023-foot summit of Haleakala.

Although each island has unique features, they share a common weather pattern. The northeasterly trade winds blow across the state, making the islands wet in the east and dry in the west. These winds pick up moisture as they cross the vast Pacific, bringing life-giving rain to Hawaii.

About the rides

The rides described in this book are arranged by island. Included are the state's six major islands: Oahu, Kauai, Lanai, Molokai, Maui, and Hawaii. Most of the rides start at community parks where you can find rest rooms, water, and parking. All of these bicycle routes are accessible without charge except for the rides in Hawaii Volcanoes National Park on the island of Hawaii and Haleakala National Park on Maui, which charge a park entrance fee.

Where possible, the rides were designed as loops that expose you to as much scenery and terrain as possible before bringing you back to the car. But due to the limited number of roads in Hawaii, many rides cover the same route out and back.

All of the rides were designed to be taken with a traditional narrow-tired road bike, although a mountain bike with slick tires will do just fine. Some roads have been poorly maintained, especially in parts of the Big Island—the island of Hawaii— where recent lava flows cover whatever asphalt is in the way. Do not use lightweight racing wheels or wheel sets with narrow rims and radially laced spokes. For these roads it's advisable to use wheels built with 14-gauge stainless-steel spokes, wide rims, and wide tires.

Oahu. Oahu is known as "the gathering place." There is still debate about whether or not this is a proper translation of the Hawaiian word, but it is a fact in terms of population. Oahu is home to the state capital, Honolulu. It's the island where most of the state's residents live, and it's the island with the most roads—and the most cars.

Oahu also has the most cyclists and the most bicycle shops. Bike riders on Oahu have to be especially wary of vehicles, as many roads provide little or no shoulder. If you do not feel comfortable sharing the road with cars and trucks, avoid riding on this island.

Many of the public buses on Oahu are equipped with a stainless-steel rack that can carry two bicycles. There is no extra fee for using the rack, and taking the bus is an excellent alternative to driving a car to the beginning of a bike ride. For bus routes and information call: (808) 848–4500.

Kauai. Of the major islands in the Hawaiian chain, Kauai is the most northerly and the oldest geologically. Its road system almost rings the island but falls short at the rugged Na Pali coast. The inaccessible mountains in the center of the island receive more rainfall than any other place on earth. Kauai also is well-known for Waimea Canyon, a huge erosional feature on the west side of the island.

Lanai. Lanai, smallest of the major islands, has less than 35 miles of paved roads—enough to keep you busy for two days at the most. A mountain bike will expand your riding options because dirt roads go to the highest point on the island and through abandoned pineapple fields. Lanai has no bicycle shops, so make sure your bike is in good shape before you visit, and bring tools to take care of minor repairs and flats.

Molokai. Molokai's tourism is down compared to Lanai, way down. Boat loads of tourists come to Lanai every day, while Molokai still languishes in a fish and poi (and watermelon) economy. Tourism has yet to leave its mark on Molokai. This island might well be the cyclist's paradise. Few cars plague the roads, and the points of interest are separated by reasonable bike-riding distances. Like Lanai, Molokai has no bike shops, so it's up to you to be sure your bicycle is in good working order.

Maui. After Oahu, Maui is the state's most developed island. Maui has few roads, but many of them have good shoulders. The landscape is dominated by the West Maui Mountains and the immense bulk of Mount Haleakala. Maui has many ride possibilities, but most cyclists come to the island specifically to ride the road that ascends from sea level to the summit of Haleakala.

Hawaii. Commonly called the Big Island, Hawaii is geologically the youngest island, and it's the biggest. Hawaii is best-known for its active volcano, Kilauea, and for having the highest mountains in the state, which top out above 13,000 feet. The island has relatively few roads, considering its size, and distances between communities are long.

Gearing up

A number of items are essential to enjoying your Hawaii bike ride.

Sunscreen. Without sunscreen, the intense tropical sun will burn your skin, and severe sun exposure can lead to a trip to the hospital. It's that simple—but you would be surprised at how many riders ignore this fact. Sunburn increases the time it takes to recover from a ride. You should never consider riding in Hawaii without applying a waterproof sunscreen.

Sunglasses. Sunglasses can protect your eyes from Hawaii's intense sunlight and from gusting winds. It doesn't take much to blind you as you speed down a steep road, and seeing what's up front is critically important, especially around motor vehicles.

Water. Always bring a lot of water. Start each ride with at least two 28-ounce water bottles, and refill them as needed along the way. Also, there's no shame in using those large water bags that are worn on your back and sucked from with a straw. Hawaii's heat requires a cyclist to drink enough to replace what is quickly lost in sweat.

Repair kit. Always carry a spare kit. Even if you never need it, a fellow cyclist might. The kit should include two spare tubes (brand new ones are best), a patch kit, tire levers, a set of hex wrenches, and a screwdriver. If you have an inflation device that utilizes compressed carbon dioxide, be sure that it works and that you know how to use it. Otherwise, bring along the tried-and-true frame-mounted pump.

Bike lock. Bicycle thefts are common in Hawaii, and someone will likely steal your bike if it's not locked up. A lock will increase your freedom to get off your bike and roam an area on foot if it suits you. A bicycle can cost as much as a used car, and it would be a shame to have it stolen.

Special clothes. Wear cycling shorts with padded inserts in the seat area. Professional racers who ride thousands of miles every season would never think to leave their comfort to just the padding on the saddle. Cycling-specific clothing may look silly, but they are designed to wick away perspiraton. After a few hours of riding they are more comfortable to wear than a sweat-soaked T-shirt. Also, wear leather riding gloves to lessen the vibrations from the handlebars and to protect your hands from getting mauled in the event of a crash.

Riding safety

There are a few things you can do to help keep your ride free from mishap.

Inspect your bike. Always check your bike before a ride. Make sure your wheels are true and securely fastened to the frame. Test your brakes to make sure they are in working order, and replace the cables if they are old and rusty. Make sure your gears change properly, and check to see if your tires are up to pressure.

Watch the road. Scan the road ahead for changing conditions. Hawaiian roads are notorious for being smooth one minute and rough the next. Heavy rains make the roads dangerous, and potholes open up where the pavement is weak.

Be aware. It takes only a momentary lapse in concentration for you to get into a dangerous situation. Keep your guard up for motorists who do not see you or who behave aggressively toward you. It's safest to ride with other people, because you are more likely to be seen, and your riding partners can help you if your bike breaks down or if you take a spill.

Avoid parked cars. City bicycle messengers know what it means to get "doored." It happens when a cyclist is riding past a row of parked cars just as a motorist inside one of the vehicles opens the front door. The result is injury for the cyclist who smashes into the open door. The best bet is to steer clear of parked cars.

Observe the law. It's common to see inexperienced cyclists riding on the wrong side of the road—against traffic instead of with it. People who do this are unlikely to survive long enough to become experienced cyclists. Besides being unsafe, riding against traffic is illegal. Obey stop signs and traffic signals, and avoid riding on sidewalks unless specifically instructed to do so by bikeway signs.

Riding on the sidewalks in Waikiki and downtown Honolulu is illegal, and the police will ticket you if they catch you doing it. Generally, if you stick to the streets it reduces the chance of your seriously injuring a pedestrian.

Be visible. First of all, avoid riding at night whenever possible. If you do ride at night, your bike is required by law to be equipped with a front headlight visible from 500 away, a red rear reflector, and reflectors visible from the side of your bike. Keep in mind, however, that motorists can still fail to see a cyclist at night even when the bicycle has a full set of reflectors and a headlight. Try to wear bright clothing no matter when you are riding, day or night.

Wear a helmet. Helmets minimize injuries to the head. If you are wearing a helmet, you have a better chance of surviving a crash that results in a blow to the head. Helmets are not required by law in Hawaii, but the law of common sense requires that you wear one.

For additional information about riding in Hawaii, contact:
Hawaii Bicycling League
P.O. Box 4403
Honolulu, HI 96812
(808) 735–5756

Sea Heaven
Lanikai and the Mokulua Islands

Number of miles:	17.0
Approximate pedaling time:	2.5 hours
Terrain:	Rolling hills
Traffic:	Heavy traffic on Kalanianaole and Kamehameha Highways
Things to see:	White sand beaches of Kailua; Mokulua Islands; Popoia Island
Food:	Meals and snacks at Windward City Shopping Center and in Kailua
Facilities:	Rest rooms and water at Kailua Beach Park and Windward City Shopping Center

Views of brilliant white sand beaches and the sparkling aqua-blue waters off the coast of Kailua are just two of the many reasons to take this ride, which includes the short but lovely Lanikai bike path.

The name Lanikai literally means "sea heaven." The area was given its name in 1924 by a land developer with the idea that the word meant "heavenly sea"—but this translation reflects English, not Hawaiian, word order. The area was known to Hawaiians as Kaohao ("the tying") because two women were said to have been tied up here after losing an ancient Hawaiian game called konane.

To get to Lanikai, start at the Windward City Shopping Center, then ride Kaneohe Bay Drive under the H-3 freeway and past the Mokapu Peninsula. Hawaiians cherished this area for its fishponds. Nowadays, the peninsula is home to a U.S. Marine base and is off limits to the general public.

Crossing a small bridge and turning onto Mokulua Drive is your signal that you are about to enter Lanikai. Mokulua Drive is named for the two islands that sit peacefully in the calm blue waters off Lanikai. The islands now serve as bird sanctuaries.

After cresting a small hill, veer right onto the Lanikai bike path on Aalapapa Drive. The path makes a loop through the quiet tree-lined neighborhood of Lanikai. A wide bike lane, light one-way traffic, and soft rolling hills make this area a favorite for in-line skaters, joggers, and cyclists.

Before leaving Lanikai on Mokulua Drive, look between the houses for the public pathways to Lanikai Beach. From the beach you can get a clear view of the Mokulua Islands. Also be sure to pull over at the scenic viewpoint on Mokulua Drive for a look at Kailua Beach and at the flat island named Popoia, which means "fish rot." The island may have received its name from fish bones that were left there.

The route returning to the Windward City Shopping Center takes you through downtown Kailua. The rhythms of an ocean-side lifestyle make Kailua a mellow place even though it has its share of development.

Once you pass the town and begin climbing up Kailua Road, the scenery is dominated by Konahuanui, at 3,150 feet the highest point in the Koolau Range. Moist trade winds from the northeast blow up against these mountains, where they cool, condense, and fall as drops of precious rain. Oahu's windward coast, including the Kailua area, thus owes its lush vegetation to the Koolaus.

Kalanianaole Highway presents the biggest uphill challenge of the day. The highway, cut into the mountain, passes an abandoned drive-in theater. Cycling uphill on this road is a slow grind, but the shoulder is generous.

You'll make a right turn onto Kamehameha Highway, which provides another good look at the Koolau Range. This highway dips under the H-3 freeway, passes two graveyards, and makes a nice descent before returning you to Kaneohe Bay Drive and the shopping center.

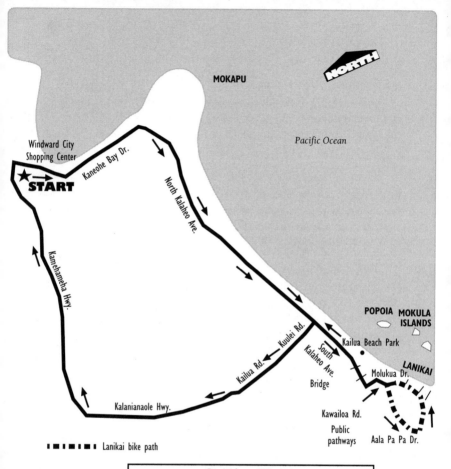

NORTH

MOKAPU

Pacific Ocean

Windward City
Shopping Center

Kaneohe Bay Dr.

★ START

North Kalaheo Ave.

Kamehameha Hwy.

POPOIA MOKULA
ISLANDS

Kailua Beach Park

Kuulei Rd.

Kailua Rd.

South Kalaheo Ave.
Bridge

LANIKAI

Molukua Dr.

Kalanianaole Hwy.

Kawailoa Rd.
Public
pathways

Aala Pa Pa Dr.

∎ ∎ ∎ ∎ ∎ Lanikai bike path

Getting There

Traveling on the H-1 freeway on the Honolulu
side of Oahu, take the Likelike Highway exit
(exit 20A). Follow the highway through the
Koolau Mountains into Kaneohe. Once you
are past three traffic lights, you will reach the
beginning of Kaneohe Bay Drive. Windward
City Shopping Center will be on the right.

DIREC-TIONS at a glance

0.0   Start on Kaneohe Bay Drive in front of the Windward City Shopping Center.

1.8   Turn left, staying on Kaneohe Bay Drive, which later becomes North Kalaheo Avenue, then South Kalaheo Avenue.

6.9   Cross the bridge onto Kawailoa Road.

7.1   Turn left onto Mokulua Drive.

7.4   Turn right onto Aalapapa Drive, where the Lanikai bike path begins.

8.5   Make a sharp left back onto Mokulua Drive where the bike path continues until you exit Lanikai.

10.0   Turn right onto Kawailoa Road.

10.2   Cross the bridge onto South Kalaheo Avenue.

11.0   Turn left onto Kuulei Road, which later becomes Kailua Road, then Kalanianaole Highway.

14.7   Turn right onto Kamehameha Highway.

17.0   Turn right onto Kaneohe Bay Drive.

Pedaling for Pearl
Arizona Memorial

Number of miles:	10.6
Approximate pedaling time:	1.5 hours
Terrain:	Flat
Traffic:	Protected bike path, but crosses several busy streets
Things to see:	Pearl Harbor, Arizona Memorial, Bowfin Memorial, Waiau power station, taro patches
Food:	Meals at the Marina Restaurant (near Ford Island Bridge) and at nearby Pearlridge Center
Facilities:	Rest rooms at the Arizona Memorial

On any given day at Pearl Harbor, delicate winds blow in from the northeast, and the land and sea meet with a soothing gentleness. The peaceful surroundings make it hard to realize that on December 7, 1941, Japanese planes sank or damaged nineteen ships in the harbor, resulting in some 2,395 deaths and pulling the United States into World War II.

To get a feel for the history of Pearl Harbor, visit the Arizona and Bowfin Memorials, which are located next to each other, then ride the bike path along the shore. The path begins at the parking lot of the Arizona Memorial, and it heads northeast away from the memorial entrance and under Ford Island Bridge. The path passes through the parking lot of the boathouse assigned to the commander in chief of the U.S. Pacific fleet. Here, a sign requests that you walk your bike because of the uneven pavement and speed bumps.

Once past the boathouse, the path continues through a grove of dry kiawe trees and up a small rise, where it crosses McGrew Loop. Along the path, thorny kiawe gives way to wild shrubs and an occasional banana tree.

At the 2-mile point, the path crosses busy Hekaha Street, enters Neal Blaisdell Park, and passes next to Hawaiian Electric Company's Waiau power plant. Next door to the power plant, a Hawaiian garden flourishes. With its sparkling irrigated patches of green taro and watercress, the garden is a study in contrast against the huge smokestacks of the power station. Taro is the plant used to make poi.

Stay on the path until it crosses Lehua Avenue at 3.6 miles. Lehua is the name of a flower that plays a central role in many Hawaiian songs and legends, and the famous blossom is often woven into leis. Cross Lehua Avenue, and look for resumption of the marked bike bath on the other side.

The path skirts an electrical substation, but then it straightens out and crosses Pearl City Peninsula, affording views of the Waianae Mountains in the distance. The path ends a mile later when it intersects with Waipio Point Access Road on the Waipio Peninsula.

Turn left onto the access road and continue until you see the Naval Inactive Ship Maintenance Facility on your left. The facility is closed to the public, but through the fence you can see long cables extending from shore to the ships. The cables carry electric current that helps protect the ships from corrosion in the tropical climate. Waipio means "curved water," and you can almost imagine the water curving inward to protect the silent ships.

To return to the Arizona Memorial parking lot, turn around and retrace your route.

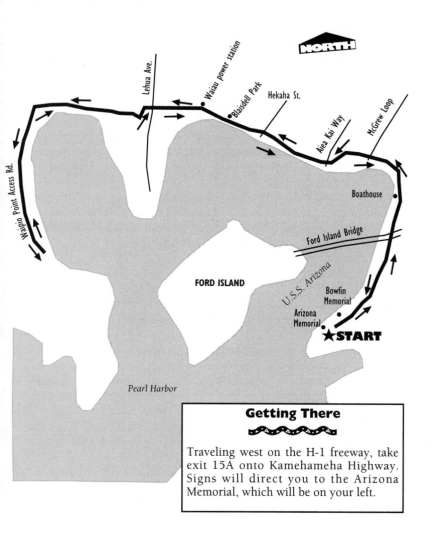

NORTH

Lehua Ave.

Waiau power station

Blaisdell Park

Hekaha St.

Aiea Kai Way

McGrew Loop

Waipio Point Access Rd.

Boathouse

Ford Island Bridge

U.S.S. Arizona

FORD ISLAND

Bowfin Memorial

Arizona Memorial

★ START

Pearl Harbor

Getting There

Traveling west on the H-1 freeway, take exit 15A onto Kamehameha Highway. Signs will direct you to the Arizona Memorial, which will be on your left.

DIREC-TIONS at a glance

0.0 Exit the Arizona Memorial parking lot heading northeast.

0.2 Pass under Ford Island Bridge.

0.5 Protected bike path begins and passes the boathouse of the commander in chief of the U.S. Pacific fleet.

1.0 Bike path crosses McGrew Loop.

1.3 Path crosses Aiea Kai Way.

2.0 Path crosses Hekaha Street.

2.4 Path enters Neal Blaisdell Park.

2.9 Path passes the Waiau power station.

3.6 Cross Lehua Avenue; bike path resumes on the other side.

5.0 Bike path ends; turn left onto Waipio Point Access Road.

5.3 Turn around at the Naval Inactive Ship Maintenance Facility. Retrace your route to return to the Arizona Memorial parking lot.

Into the Vast Valley
Manoa Valley and the University of Hawaii

Number of miles:	6.8
Approximate pedaling time:	1 hour
Terrain:	Mostly flat
Traffic:	Light traffic on weekends; weekdays are busy
Things to see:	University of Hawaii's Manoa campus, Manoa Valley, a Chinese cemetery, Lyon Arboretum, fishponds, tropical jungle
Food:	Meals and snacks at Manoa Marketplace, Campus Center, and on East Manoa Road

Rainbows form so frequently in Manoa Valley that they are seldom noticed by the average resident. Tucked into the Koolau Mountains, Manoa Valley is kept lush and green by the frequent passing rain showers.

Start your ride into Manoa Valley from Jefferson Hall at the University of Hawaii. Founded in 1907, the university moved from downtown Honolulu into residential Manoa in 1912 and has been growing ever since. Today some 20,000 students are enrolled.

Use the emergency fire road to leave the campus. The fire road is locked to motor vehicles, but a gate allows pedestrians and bicycles to pass through. The fire road is short, and half of it is graveled. At the end of the fire road, turn left, back onto the pavement, and continue riding toward the back of the valley on Pamoa Road.

The view of the valley from Woodlawn Drive, at 1.1 miles, makes it easy to understand how Manoa received its name,

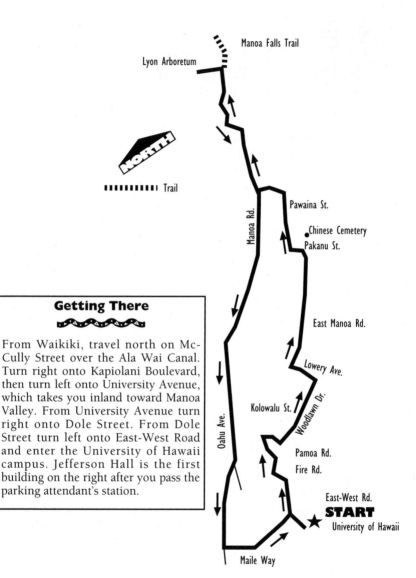

Manoa Falls Trail

Lyon Arboretum

NORTH

||||||||||| Trail

Pawaina St.

Manoa Rd.

Chinese Cemetery
Pakanu St.

East Manoa Rd.

Lowery Ave.

Kolowalu St.

Woodlawn Dr.

Oahu Ave.

Pamoa Rd.
Fire Rd.

East-West Rd.
START
University of Hawaii

Maile Way

Getting There

From Waikiki, travel north on Mc-Cully Street over the Ala Wai Canal. Turn right onto Kapiolani Boulevard, then turn left onto University Avenue, which takes you inland toward Manoa Valley. From University Avenue turn right onto Dole Street. From Dole Street turn left onto East-West Road and enter the University of Hawaii campus. Jefferson Hall is the first building on the right after you pass the parking attendant's station.

DIRECTIONS at a glance

0.0 From Jefferson Hall on the University of Hawaii campus, head north on East-West Road.

0.3 Stay on East-West Road as it turns sharply to the left.

0.4 Turn right from East-West Road onto the emergency fire road.

0.5 From the fire road, turn left onto Pamoa Road.

0.6 After the stop sign, turn right, staying on Pamoa Road.

0.7 After the stop sign, turn right onto Kolowalu Street; Kolowalu becomes Woodlawn Drive.

1.2 Turn left onto Lowery Avenue.

1.3 At the light, turn right onto East Manoa Road.

1.8 East Manoa Road forks; veer onto the left fork of East Manoa.

1.9 Turn left onto Pakanu Street.

2.0 Turn right onto Pawaina Street.

2.5 Turn right onto Manoa Road.

2.8 Manoa Road becomes steep as it narrows and curves tightly.

3.2 Manoa Road ends and Manoa Falls trail begins.

3.4 Turn around at the Lyon Arboretum parking lot, and return to Manoa Road.

5.1 From the five-way stop on Manoa Road, take the second left onto Oahu Avenue.

5.8 After the traffic light, stay to the right to stay on Oahu Avenue.

6.1 Turn left onto Maile Way, and continue straight through the intersection to return to the University of Hawaii.

6.7 Turn right onto East-West Road.

6.8 Turn left to return to Jefferson Hall.

which means "vast" in Hawaiian. Green mountains stand well-away from the valley's wide interior section. The mountains frequently send down wispy curtains of rain that seem perfect for forming rainbows.

The next point of interest is the beautifully landscaped Chinese cemetery, at 1.9 miles. The cemetery and its willow trees are situated on a gentle hill overlooking the valley.

As you approach the back of the valley on Manoa Road, the grade steepens. Use caution as you approach this section because the road becomes so twisted and narrow that it's difficult to see around the turns. Toward the end of the road you will enter a jungle with moist air, vines, and towering trees. Paradise Park used to welcome visitors along this road, but since closing of the park, the jungle has been working steadily to reclaim the pavilion that was built there.

At the end of Manoa Road, you can explore the hiking trail to Manoa Falls, and you can visit Lyon Arboretum. The trail features a popular 0.8-mile walk to one of Manoa's beautiful waterfalls. The arboretum's extensive plant collection, including some 600 varieties of palms, is open to the public from 9 A.M. to 3 P.M. every day except Sunday. The ride to the arboretum parking lot is a short climb up a steep, curving driveway. Once at the top and above the jungle canopy, you are greeted with a spectacular view of the base of the Koolau Range.

To return to the university, ride down Manoa Road to a five-way intersection, where you'll find a choice of two roads on your left. Take the second left, onto Oahu Avenue. At 5.8 miles into your day's ride, bear to the right to stay on Oahu Avenue. If you go to the left, you will end up on a narrow, dangerous section of University Avenue.

Next, turn left from Oahu Avenue onto Maile Way, named after a vine with fragrant shiny leaves that is often used to make leis for important occasions like graduations or weddings. In another three-quarters of a mile, you'll be back at your starting point.

To unwind after the ride, visit the quiet fishponds and ornamented garden behind Jefferson Hall.

4 Pedaling to Cool Heights
Nuuanu Pali Lookout

Number of miles:	9.9
Approximate pedaling time:	2 hours
Terrain:	Low-grade hill; some steep sections
Traffic:	Heavy on weekdays; light on weekend mornings
Things to see:	Panoramic views of Oahu's windward coast, tropical rain forest, peaceful lily ponds, Queen Emma's Summer Palace
Food:	Snacks at Nuuanu Plaza on Nuuanu Avenue and at Laimi Mini Mart
Facilities:	Rest rooms and water at Nuuanu Valley Park

Riding to the Pali Lookout offers the chance to see a wonderful view of Oahu's windward coast, and on the way it also gives you a good look at Nuuanu Valley's lush tropical rain forest. In Hawaiian, "nuuanu" means "cool height." Queen Emma, wife of Kamehameha IV, retreated to Nuuanu during the summer months. Her house is now a museum (808–595–3167). The land surrounding her house was turned into Nuuanu Valley Park.

Start the ride from Nuuanu Valley Park, turning left onto Puiwa Road. Puiwa means "startled" in Hawaiian. During a 1795 battle, King Kamehameha used guns instead of traditional weapons, and this startled his enemies.

After passing through a quiet neighborhood on Dowsett Avenue, the route turns onto Nuuanu Pali Drive, a remnant of the old Pali Highway. This road sees less traffic than the new high-

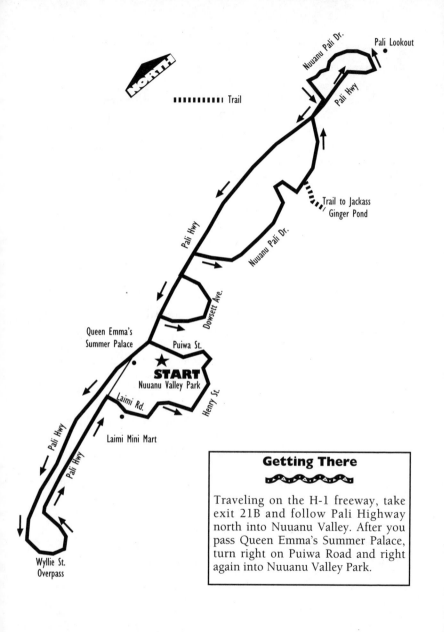

NORTH

▪▪▪▪▪▪▪▪▪▪▪ Trail

Pali Lookout

Nuuanu Pali Dr.

Pali Hwy

Trail to Jackass
Ginger Pond

Nuuanu Pali Dr.

Pali Hwy

Dowsett Ave.

Queen Emma's
Summer Palace

Puiwa St.

★ START
Nuuanu Valley Park

Henry St.

Laimi Rd.

Laimi Mini Mart

Pali Hwy

Pali Hwy

Wyllie St.
Overpass

Getting There

Traveling on the H-1 freeway, take
exit 21B and follow Pali Highway
north into Nuuanu Valley. After you
pass Queen Emma's Summer Palace,
turn right on Puiwa Road and right
again into Nuuanu Valley Park.

DIREC-TIONS at a glance

0.0 From the Nuuanu Valley Park parking lot, turn left onto Puiwa Road; then at the traffic light, turn right onto the Pali Highway.

0.1 Turn right onto Dowsett Avenue. Follow Dowsett until it ends.

0.7 At the end of Dowsett, turn right and merge back onto the Pali Highway.

0.8 Before the traffic light, bear right onto Nuuanu Pali Drive.

2.5 Turn right and continue on the Pali Highway. The shoulder narrows as you approach the Pali Lookout. Strong headwinds are common.

3.8 At the sign, take the Pali Lookout cutoff just before the tunnels.

4.0 Stop to explore the Nuuanu Pali Lookout. When you exit the lookout, take the Honolulu-bound exit onto Nuuanu Pali Drive.

5.0 After the stop sign, turn right onto the Pali Highway.

8.3 Turn left onto the Wyllie Street overpass.

8.4 Merge back onto the Pali Highway heading north.

8.9 Turn right onto Laimi Road.

9.2 Turn left onto Henry Street.

9.3 Turn left onto Puiwa Road.

9.9 Turn left into Nuuanu Valley Park.

way, and it features vine-laden trees that form a green tunnel over the mossy roadway. Once under the trees, Nuuanu Pali Drive begins to twist and curve, and the faint sound of gurgling water can be heard from Nuuanu Stream.

Nuuanu Pali Drive passes a popular swimming pond called Kahuailanawai ("site of tranquil water"). But most people know the pond simply as Jackass Ginger, the name it was given in the early 1900s for a donkey that was tied up near the pond and for the yellow ginger flowers that grow all around. Look to the right of the road for the trail going down to the pond. The trail is visible shortly after you travel through a series of tight S-turns.

The next point of interest is the Board of Water Supply's pumping station, situated on your left. The manicured lawn in front of the station welcomes a picnic, and the lily ponds and nearby creek are fun to explore. Behind the station is one of four reservoirs in the valley that collect rainwater from Nuuanu's frequent showers.

The steepest and most difficult part of the ride comes directly after the pumping station. If you can make the half-mile climb to the end of Nuuanu Pali Drive, you will find the rest of the ride comparatively easy.

At the end of Nuuanu Pali Drive, turn right and continue up the Pali Highway. Along the right side of the valley are the twin peaks of Konahuanui, highest points in the Koolaus. Hawaiian legend has it that the two peaks were formed when a monster, assigned to block the pass at the top of Nuuanu, threw his genitals down in disgust after realizing an old woman had slipped past him.

Once on the Pali Highway, the shoulders slowly narrow, and you may find yourself fighting a headwind. At the 3.8-mile point on your ride, veer right and follow the cutoff to the Nuuanu Pali Lookout. The word "pali" means "cliff." In 1795, Nuuanu Valley was the site of Kamehameha's final battle to unify the Hawaiian Islands. Some 300 Oahu warriors were either pushed off Nuuanu Pali or jumped to their death rather than surrender to Kamehameha.

Nuuanu Pali Lookout is often windy because it's a low point on the Koolau Range, and the towering green mountains on either side funnel the trade winds swiftly through the pass. As the wind blows though your helmet, you can enjoy a spectacular panoramic view that includes the mountains and Oahu's windward coast.

To return to Nuuanu Valley Park, take the Honolulu-bound exit, which is the last section of the old highway. Use caution, as this stretch is poorly maintained and frequently is mossy and wet. It meets up again with the Pali Highway a mile later. Turn right onto the highway and hold on tight for a high-speed descent to the Wyllie Street overpass.

The return trip is uphill on Pali Highway and includes a short tour though a residential subdivision before returning to the shady trees of Nuuanu Valley Park.

Tantalized
Tantalus Drive

Number of miles:	11
Approximate pedaling time:	1.5 hours
Terrain:	Hill, with some steep sections
Traffic:	Light
Things to see:	Puu Ualakaa State Wayside Park; the Contemporary Museum; sweeping views of Makiki Valley, Diamond Head, and Punchbowl Crater (National Memorial Cemetery of the Pacific)
Food:	Cafe at the Contemporary Museum; snacks at Makiki Shopping Village
Facilities:	Rest rooms at Puu Ualakaa State Park

From crowded Waikiki, it's easy to exchange towering hotels, cars, and concrete for wild ginger blossoms, cool mountain mist, and lush vegetation. Just take a spin up Tantalus.

Standing behind busy Honolulu, Tantalus is a mountain that draws outdoor enthusiasts from all over the island. Incredible views of Honolulu, Makiki Valley, Manoa Valley, Punchbowl Crater, and Diamond Head make it well worth the effort to bicycle up the mountain. Add in the Contemporary Museum and Puu Ualakaa State Wayside Park, and this becomes a ride you cannot afford to miss.

The ride is a loop with about 5 miles of climbing and 6 miles of downhill cruising. The ride starts and ends in Makiki, a valley named for the type of stones found there. Hawaiians used these stones as weights for their octopus lures.

Starting from Makiki Heights Drive near the Board of Water

Supply's Makiki pumping station, head north toward the mountain. At first the road seems gentle, but it quickly rises into steady switchbacks until you reach the Contemporary Museum at 1.3 miles. The peaceful museum features a cafe and guided tours. Its mission is to showcase mixed-media artwork from 1940 to present. Local artists are often featured at the museum. Before it became a museum, it was a private estate owned by the prominent Spalding family. The museum's hours vary, so call for times and tour schedules (808–526–0232).

Your route goes up Makiki Heights Drive until it intersects with Tantalus Drive, where you'll turn onto Tantalus to continue the climb. At 1.9 miles, stop at the viewpoint, and treat yourself to the views of Makiki Valley and Diamond Head Crater.

You'll soon hit the steepest section of Tantalus Drive, but only two-tenths of a mile later the road flattens out, allowing you to recover enough to enjoy the view down into Punchbowl Crater, home of the National Memorial Cemetery of the Pacific.

With the toughest part of the ride behind you and the smell of eucalyptus trees in the air, Tantalus Drive presents broad, sweeping switchbacks until it nears the top. For a brief section before the top, the road climbs sharply, then narrows to one lane. Watch for cars coming the other way. At the top, the sweet smell of ginger blossoms encourages every pedal stroke. Here, Tantalus Drive turns into Round Top Drive.

Take the first part of the descent with extra care. It's steep and narrow. Gradually the road gets wider, and it becomes easier to carve a line down the mountain. At the 7.5-mile point on your ride, stop by Puu Ualakaa State Wayside Park. (Puu Ualakaa translates literally as "rolling sweet potato hill.") The park offers bathroom facilities, plus a spectacular viewpoint that allows you to see from Manoa Valley and Diamond Head all the way to the distant Waianae Mountains.

At the bottom of Round Top Drive, turn right onto Makiki Street, then right again to complete the loop onto Makiki Heights Drive.

Top

Narrow
Section

Round Top Dr.

Tantalus Dr.

Puu Ualakaa State
Wayside Park

Manoa
Valley Lookout

Contemporary
Museum

Makiki Hts. Dr.

START

Makiki St.

Getting There

From Waikiki, travel north on McCully Street, which becomes Metcalf Street after crossing over the H-1 freeway. Turn left onto Wilder Avenue. Pass Punahou school and the YMCA on the right, then turn right onto Makiki Street. From Makiki Street, turn left onto Makiki Heights Drive. Street parking is on the left across from the Makiki pumping station.

DIREC-TIONS at a glance

0.0 From the Makiki pumping station, go north on Makiki Heights Drive.

1.6 Stop and turn right onto Tantalus Drive.

2.4 Begin the steep section.

2.6 View Punchbowl Crater (national cemetery) through eucalyptus trees on the left. The steep section ends.

4.4 Negotiate narrow single-lane roadway.

4.8 Reach the summit, and carefully descend steep downhill section. Tantalus Drive becomes Round Top Drive.

7.5 Turn right to Puu Ualakaa State Wayside Park.

7.8 Bathroom facilities and viewpoint are located on park's summit.

8.0 Turn around, and leave the park by the way you came in.

8.5 Turn right onto Round Top Drive.

10.7 Turn right onto Makiki Street.

11.0 Turn right onto Makiki Heights Drive.

6 Exploring the Protected Bay
Honolulu and the Harbor

Number of miles:	24.1
Approximate pedaling time:	2.5 hours
Terrain:	Mostly flat
Traffic:	Very heavy on weekday mornings, lighter on weekends
Things to see:	Kakaako Waterfront Park, Kewalo Basin, State Capitol Building, Iolani Palace, King Kamehameha statue, Chinatown, Honolulu Harbor, Aloha Tower
Food:	Meals and snacks in downtown Honolulu, Chinatown, and Aloha Tower Market Place
Facilities:	Rest rooms and water at Kakaako Waterfront Park

Honolulu means "protected bay" in Hawaiian, and until airplanes could fly to Hawaii, everything arrived by ship. It was because of Oahu's excellent protected bay that Honolulu became the capital of Hawaii.

Throughout the years, construction industries, agricultural producers, and a garbage dump claimed the land close to the harbor, allowing its beauty to be obscured and forgotten. But thanks to newly constructed parks, bike lanes, and a renewed interest in Oahu's waterfront, it's once again possible to enjoy the beauty of Honolulu Harbor.

Start the ride at Kakaako Waterfront Park. The park's rolling hills and green grass cover what was once a garbage dump. Views of Waikiki Beach and Kewalo Basin are possible from the park. In

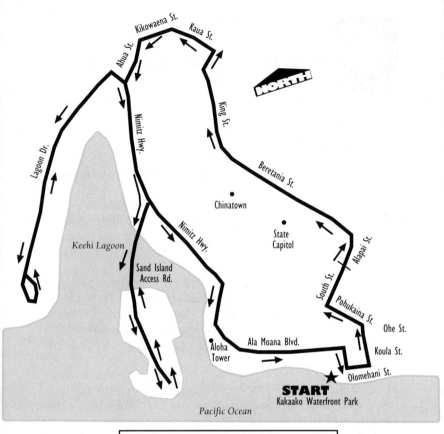

Getting There

From Waikiki, take Ala Moana Boulevard east. Pass Ala Moana Shopping Center and Ward Warehouse on your right. Turn left onto Koula Street then right onto Olomehani Street, which leads directly to Kakaako Waterfront Park.

DIREC-TIONS at a glance

0.0 Turn right from Kakaako Waterfront Park onto Olomehani Street.

0.1 Turn left onto Koula Street.

0.6 Turn left onto Pohukaina Street.

0.9 Turn right onto South Street, which later becomes Alapai Street. Stay to the left.

1.5 Turn left onto Beretania Street; stay on left-hand side.

1.8 Stop to explore the State Capitol Building, Iolani Palace, and the statue of King Kamehameha I.

2.3 Beretania Street becomes two-way; move to right-hand side of the road.

2.5 Turn right onto King Street.

4.5 King Street crosses over H-1 freeway and ends; turn left onto Kaua Street. Riding on the sidewalk is allowed.

5.2 Bear left onto Kikowaena Street; ride bridge over H-1 freeway.

5.4 Turn left onto Ahua Street.

6.1 Turn right onto Nimitz Highway bike path.

6.3 Turn left onto Lagoon Drive, using crosswalk.

8.6 Turn around at the end of Lagoon Drive, and retrace your route back to Nimitz Highway.

11.0 Turn right onto Nimitz Highway.

13.7 Turn right onto Sand Island Access Road; follow bike path across Sand Island Bridge, and continue until you reach Sand Island State Recreation Area.

17.2 Turn around at Sand Island State Recreation Area, and retrace your route back to Nimitz Highway.

20.7 Turn right from Sand Island Access Road onto Nimitz Highway, which later becomes Ala Moana Boulevard.

23.8 Turn right onto Ohe Street.

24.1 Return to Kakaako Waterfront Park.

ancient Hawaii, the Kewalo area was a site of human sacrifice where society's outcasts were drowned; these days it's known for excellent surfing. When the surf is up, wave riders take daring runs close to the rocks at a break known as Point Panic.

After passing through the Kakaako area, ride into downtown Honolulu, where a variety of sights appear within a one-block area. You can lock your bike at the racks behind the State Capitol Building or in front of the State Library. Now is your chance to explore the reflecting pools at the capitol or to take a walking tour of Iolani Palace, the only royal palace in the United States. Cross King Street to visit the statue of Kamehameha I, the Hawaiian king who unified the islands.

After your walking tour, return to Beretania Street, and stay on the left-hand side to pass by Fort Street Mall, the lei-making shops on Maunakea Street, and Chinatown. Up to this point, Beretania Street is open to one-way traffic, but then it becomes two-way; carefully make your way to the right-hand side of the road.

Once on King Street, you will enter the Kalihi area, where faded cinder-block buildings replace the glass and steel towers of downtown. Cross the H-1 freeway overpass and turn left onto Kaua Street, where riding on the sidewalk is permitted after you pass Middle Street. You'll get off the sidewalk to bear left onto the Kikowaena Street bridge that takes you into the Mapunapuna industrial area, a part of Hawaii you will not see in tourist brochures. The streets are lined with construction suppliers, warehouses, lumber yards, and heavy equipment. Strategically located between the harbor and the airport, many businesses have made Mapunapuna their center of operations.

Leaving Mapunapuna, ride onto Lagoon Drive, where unobstructed views of Honolulu await. From this vantage point, you can see the entire city skyline with the misty green Koolau Mountains rising beyond. Airplanes taking off from the nearby international airport thunder overhead, drowning out the occasional sound of lapping water from nearby Keehi Lagoon.

Before returning to town, take a ride out Sand Island Access Road. The road takes you over a bridge, past the Matson shipyard, and into the Sand Island State Recreation Area. Occupied primarily by busy shipyards, equipment shops, and construction suppliers, Sand Island is the last place you would expect to find a park. But the park is peaceful and relaxing, especially in comparison with downtown Honolulu, visible from the park.

On your way back into the city, stop to explore the Aloha Tower Market Place, on the right-hand side of Nimitz Highway. The marketplace was developed around Aloha Tower, the tallest building in Honolulu when it was built in 1925. Next to the marketplace is the Hawaii Maritime Museum, another exciting place to explore.

As you ride back to Kakaako Waterfront Park, Nimitz Highway changes name to Ala Moana Boulevard. Shortly before the park, turn right onto Ohe Street, which is easy to miss because it's unmarked and tightly nestled between two car dealerships. Ohe Street takes you directly back to the rolling green hills of the waterfront park.

Search for Spouting Water
Waikiki

Number of miles:	13.7
Approximate pedaling time:	2 hours
Terrain:	Hills near Diamond Head and Makiki, otherwise flat
Traffic:	Heavy traffic
Things to see:	Magic Island, U.S. Army Museum at Fort DeRussy, statue of Duke Kahanamoku, Honolulu Zoo, Waikiki Aquarium, Diamond Head Crater, Ala Moana Regional Park
Food:	Meals and snacks in Waikiki, snacks at Waiola Store
Facilities:	Rest rooms and water at Ala Moana Regional Park

Waikiki means "spouting water" in Hawaiian, but these days the only spouting waters you will find are the elaborate fountains in front of towering hotels and glitzy shopping malls. Waikiki was a marshland before it was drained by the Ala Wai Canal and turned into the tourism capital of the Pacific.

A ride through the congested streets of Waikiki can be a fast-paced adventure. But if you ride on the weekends in early morning, when the streets are less crowded, you can see Waikiki at your own pace. Bring a bicycle lock because there are many opportunities for leaving your bike to explore.

Start the ride at Aina Moana State Recreation Area. Locals simply call the park Magic Island. Ride across the bridge over the Ala Wai Canal and into Waikiki. On the right-hand side of Kalia Road, 1.2 miles into your ride, is the U.S. Army Museum

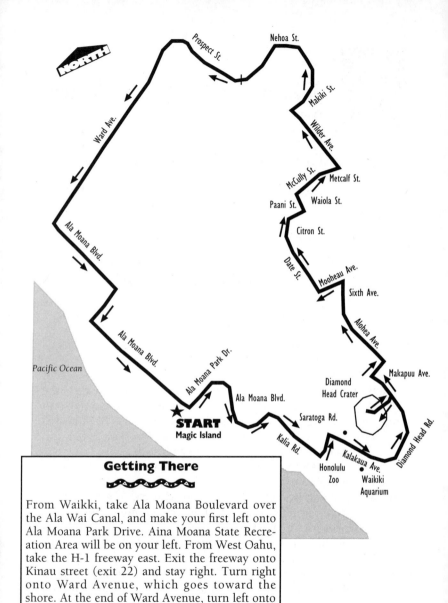

NORTH

Prospect St.

Nehoa St.

Makiki St.

Wilder Ave.

Ward Ave.

McCully St. — Metcalf St.

Paani St. — Waiola St.

Citron St.

Ala Moana Blvd.

Date St. — Mooheau Ave.

Sixth Ave.

Alohea Ave.

Ala Moana Blvd.

Makapuu Ave.

Pacific Ocean

Ala Moana Park Dr.

Diamond Head Crater

Ala Moana Blvd.

★ **START**
Magic Island

Saratoga Rd.

Kalia Rd.

Kalakaua Ave.

Diamond Head Rd.

Honolulu Zoo

Waikiki Aquarium

Getting There

From Waikki, take Ala Moana Boulevard over the Ala Wai Canal, and make your first left onto Ala Moana Park Drive. Aina Moana State Recreation Area will be on your left. From West Oahu, take the H-1 freeway east. Exit the freeway onto Kinau street (exit 22) and stay right. Turn right onto Ward Avenue, which goes toward the shore. At the end of Ward Avenue, turn left onto Ala Moana Boulevard. Turn right at the sign onto Ala Moana Park Drive. Aina Moana State Recreation Area will be on your right.

DIREC-TIONS at a glance

0.0 Start from Aina Moana State Recreation Area (Magic Island), and ride east on Ala Moana Park Drive.

0.2 Turn right onto Ala Moana Boulevard.

0.7 Turn right onto Kalia Road.

1.2 Turn left onto Saratoga Road.

1.4 Turn right onto Kalakaua Avenue.

3.1 Turn left onto Diamond Head Road.

4.5 Bear left and continue on Diamond Head Road.

5.2 Turn left onto the Diamond Head Crater access road.

5.8 Turn around at the Diamond Head trail parking lot; retrace your route to exit the crater.

6.4 Turn left onto Diamond Head Road.

6.6 Turn right onto Makapuu Avenue.

6.7 Turn left onto Alohea Avenue.

7.3 Alohea Avenue becomes Sixth Avenue.

7.5 Turn left onto Mooheau Avenue.

7.7 After the stoplight, continue straight onto Date Street.

8.8 Bear to the right onto Citron Street.

8.9 Turn right onto Paani Street.

9.0 Turn left onto Waiola Street.

9.2 Turn right onto McCully Street.

9.4 Cross McCully Street bridge; McCully becomes Metcalf Street.

9.7 Turn left onto Wilder Avenue.

10.3 Turn right onto Makiki Street.

10.5 Turn left onto Nehoa Street.

11.1 Merge right onto Prospect Street.

11.6 Turn left onto Ward Avenue.

12.8 Turn left onto Ala Moana Boulevard.

13.0 Turn right onto Ala Moana Park Drive.

13.7 Return to Aina Moana State Recreation Area (Magic Island).

at Fort DeRussy. The fort stands as a lasting reminder of the attack on the Waikiki area that was feared during World War II, but never came.

The route takes you onto Kalakaua Avenue, named after Hawaii's King Kalakaua. During the early-morning hours, the skyrise hotels cast shadows in Waikiki, and it isn't until you ride past the hotels that you get your first glimpse of Waikiki Beach and the open sky.

On the right side of the road, look for the statue of Duke Kahanamoku. A former sheriff and Olympic swimming champion, Kahanamoku is also considered by many to be the father of modern surfing. The outstretched arms of the statue are often adorned with flower leis. Before reaching the end of Kalakaua Avenue, you will also pass the Honolulu Zoo and the Waikiki Aquarium, both excellent diversions.

Turning from Kalakaua Avenue, you will begin your ascent of Diamond Head. The volcanic crater and symbol of Waikiki has long been silent, but it still looks as if it could erupt at any moment, as it did when it was violently created only 100,000 years ago. On the way to the crater's entrance, stop and enjoy the scenic viewpoint that includes the Kahala coastline and Koko Crater in the distance. A paved walkway takes you from the viewpoint to the beach below.

At 4.5 miles into this ride, Diamond Head Road forks. Bear to the left to stay on Diamond Head Road, and continue until you take a left onto the crater access road. This road takes you through a short tunnel and into the crater. Here is the beginning of a trail that goes through abandoned World War II bunkers and to the top of Leahi Peak, highest point on the crater rim.

Leave the crater the same way you came in, and continue the ride into the Moiliili area. You can sample the island's best shave ice (snow cones) at the Waiola Store, at the 9-mile point of your ride. Hidden among nondescript two-story apartments, the store serves up its shave ice in exotic flavors like mango, li hing mui, and litchi. For an extra boost of energy, order a cone with black azuke beans at the bottom.

The ride continues on rolling terrain through the densely packed apartment area of Makiki, then onto the slopes of Punchbowl Crater, before returning to the sea on Ward Avenue. You'll soon arrive at Ala Moana Regional Park, a favorite place for people to cruise next to the beach in their custom-built hot rods. The park drive leads back to Aina Moana State Recreation Area, completing your Waikiki adventure.

To the Bulging Eye Lookout
Makapuu Point

Number of miles:	24.2
Approximate pedaling time:	3 hours
Terrain:	Mostly flat with the exception of hills at Hanauma Bay, Makapuu, and Hawaii Kai Drive
Traffic:	Heavy traffic on Kalanianaole Highway, especially on weekday mornings and when the surf is up at Sandy Beach and Makapuu
Things to see:	Palm trees in Kahala, Hanauma Bay, Koko Crater, the Blowhole, Sandy Beach Park, Makapuu Lookout
Food:	Meals and snacks in Waikiki or along the route at Koko Marina Shopping Center and Kahala Mall
Facilities:	Water at Fort Ruger Park, rest rooms at Kawaikui Beach Park and Maunalua Bay Beach Park

Paint the sky blue and the sun blazing yellow. Plant palm trees and green grass at roadside beach parks. Then explode white foaming waves against rocky cliffs, and you have just created the common sights along the road to Makapuu Lookout. This is one of the most popular rides on Oahu because of its dramatic scenery and typically sunny weather. Road conditions are excellent because of the generous bike lane that extends through most of the Hawaii Kai area.

Start the ride at Fort Ruger Park behind Diamond Head. Lo-

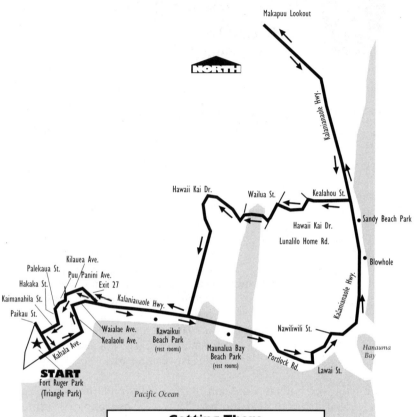

Makapuu Lookout

NORTH

Kalanianaole Hwy.

Hawaii Kai Dr.

Wailua St.

Kealahou St.

Sandy Beach Park

Hawaii Kai Dr.

Lunalilo Home Rd.

Blowhole

Kilauea Ave.

Palekaua St.

Puu Panini Ave.

Hakaka St.

Exit 27

Kaimanahila St.

Kalanianaole Hwy.

Kaʻananaole Hwy.

Paikau St.

Waialae Ave.

Kealaolu Ave.

Kawaikui Beach Park
(rest rooms)

Nawiliwili St.

Kahala Ave.

Maunalua Bay Beach Park
(rest rooms)

Portlock Rd.

Hanauma Bay

START
Fort Ruger Park
(Triangle Park)

Lawai St.

Pacific Ocean

Getting There

From Waikiki, head east on Kalakaua Avenue. At the end of Kalakaua, turn right onto Diamond Head Road. After climbing a brief hill and passing the Diamond Head Lookout on your right, look for Fort Ruger Park on the left. It's at the intersection of Diamond Head Road and Kahala Avenue.

DIREC-TIONS
at a glance

0.0	From Paikau Street next to Fort Ruger Park (Triangle Park), turn left onto Kahala Avenue
1.3	Turn left onto Kealaolu Avenue.
2.0	Turn right onto Waialae Avenue and merge onto Kalanianaole Highway.

6.9 Turn right onto Portlock Road.

7.4 Turn left onto Lawai Street.

7.6 Turn right onto Nawiliwili Street.

8.0 Turn right onto Kalanianaole Highway.

8.4 Hanauma Bay entrance is on right-hand side of the road.

10.1 Sandy Beach Park is on your right.

12.3 Makapuu Lookout; turn around and go back the way you came.

13.8 Turn right onto Kealahou Street.

14.6 Turn left onto Hawaii Kai Drive.

15.6 Turn left onto Lunalilo Home Road.

16.3 Turn right onto Wailua Street.

16.7 Turn left onto Hawaii Kai Drive.

17.0 Turn right, staying on Hawaii Kai Drive.

18.3 Turn right onto Kalanianaole Highway.

22.4 Turn right at exit 27. Do not enter the Lunalilo Freeway.

22.6 Turn left onto Kilauea Avenue at the first traffic light under the Lunalilo Freeway. Use the center lane.

23.4 Turn left onto Puu Panini Avenue.

23.8 Turn left onto Palekaua Street.

23.9 Turn left onto Hakaka Street.

24.0 Turn right onto Kaimanahila Street.

24.2 Turn right onto Paikau Street, returning to Fort Ruger Park.

cals call it Triangle Park. Ride past multimillion-dollar beach-front mansions in the Kahala area and onto Kalanianaole Highway. The well-designed bike lane and flat terrain allow for comfortable riding along the highway for the next 4.9 miles. Kawaikui Beach Park, at 4.25 miles, and Maunalua Bay Beach Park at 6 miles, are along this stretch of the coast. Both are visible from the road on the right.

After turning from Kalanianaole Highway onto Portlock Road, you'll find riding through the quiet Portlock neighborhood a welcome relief from the busy thoroughfare. This stretch also allows you to gather strength for ascending the hill between Hanauma Bay and Koko Crater.

At a point 8.4 miles into this ride, you pass the entrance to Hanauma Bay, created thousands of years ago when a volcanic crater partially collapsed into the sea and became flooded with water. It's now a marine sanctuary and a popular place to snorkel because of its calm waters and abundant reef fish.

After passing Hanauma Bay and a spectacular view of Koko Crater, Kalanianaole Highway narrows and follows the coastline on top of rocky sea cliffs. The Pacific Ocean sparkles below in the intense sunlight and periodically sends a wall of water exploding into white foam against the rocks below. Stopping at the Blowhole viewpoint is a must. Here, the ocean sprays a gigantic fountain of water into the air from a large hole in the rocks. On a clear day you can see Molokai, Lanai, and Maui from the lookout.

Kalanianaole Highway drops down to sea level near Sandy Beach Park. Ocean enthusiasts flock to this beach to bodysurf the famous shore breaks. Beyond the beach, the area is barren and hot, with only scrub grass growing among dirt and rocks.

About 2 miles beyond Sandy Beach, the highway begins to climb toward Makapuu Point. The ride can be difficult at the beginning of the hill, where cyclists frequently are greeted with a blast of wind in the face. From Makapuu Lookout, you can see the beaches along Oahu's windward coast and across to the nearby tiny islands of Manana and Kaohikaipu. One translation for Makapuu is "bulging eye," but this is not for the wonderful view. Rather, it is named after a rock that looks like an eye. The rock is located in a cave that can be seen only from the sea just off Makapuu Point. The cave is also said to be the dwelling of a hungry goddess.

From the lookout, return along Kalanianaole Highway to the Hawaii Kai area, turning right on Kealahou Street. You will find the return ride along Kalanianaole Highway much easier because the trade winds tend to blow in this direction. You'll encounter a half-mile-long hill on Hawaii Kai Drive. The route then returns to Kalanianaole Highway for another 4 miles. Take exit 27 from the highway in order to get onto Kilauea Avenue. After rolling by Kahala Mall, you will return to the plush Kahala neighborhood and to Fort Ruger Park.

Sand and Sky
Mokuleia

Number of miles:	14.8
Approximate pedaling time:	2 hours
Terrain:	Flat
Traffic:	Light on weekdays, heavier on weekends
Things to see:	Mokuleia Beach Park, Waianae Mountains, Dillingham Airfield and Gliderport, skydivers, windsurfers
Food:	Snacks at Thompson Corner, meals in nearby Haleiwa and Wahiawa
Facilities:	Rest rooms and water at Mokuleia Beach Park

If you yearn for peaceful surroundings, a ride to Mokuleia is the perfect solution. Mokuleia is the escape from the hustle and bustle of downtown Honolulu, and the beaches at Mokuleia are far less crowded than those at Waikiki.

The ride is a simple out and back on Farrington Highway starting from Waialua Intermediate and High School. Although the roadway is fairly narrow, it does not have a great deal of traffic because it dead-ends. The road used to continue around rugged Kaena Point, but it has not been maintained for many years, and now it's difficult to even walk the old route.

Generous amounts of sun, surf, wind, and sand are heaped onto this part of Oahu. Be sure to bring a lot of water as it gets very hot, especially near Kaena Point.

The ride starts off with little hint of what is to come. The trades normally provide a tailwind, and the road flows along flat and smooth beneath your wheels. From the outskirts of Waialua all you see are sugarcane fields and modest plantation cottages. On the left are the steep green cliffs of the Waianae Range. The beach seems far away, but only 4.4 miles down the road you come upon Mokuleia Beach Park. A small sand dune beyond the parking lot hides a beautiful beach.

Skin divers frequent the ocean here in the mornings or during periods of low surf. And later in the day, if a strong breeze develops, windsurfers take to the sea. With a deceptively simple hop on their boards and a skillful twist of the sails, windsurfers harness the power of the wind to take them on blindingly quick rides from the shore out to sea and back again.

After Mokuleia Beach Park, Farrington Highway follows the shoreline, passing the YMCA's Camp Erdman, until the pavement ends at 7.5 miles. Use caution along the way to avoid slippery patches of sand that are sometimes washed onto the road.

Beyond the pavement lies Kaena Point, which literally means "the heat." Kaena marks one end of the Waianae Range, and as the mountains descend to the point, they lose their green color until finally they are covered with only a few hardy scrubs able to cope in the arid climate. Kaena Point is frequently the hottest place on Oahu.

Turn around where the pavement ends and retrace your route for a mile and a half, where you can turn right into Dillingham Airfield and Gliderport, open to the public between 7 A.M. and 6 P.M. The airfield roadway takes you past a small-aircraft hangar, then parallel to the airfield to a staging area. Gliders are towed from the airfield into the sky, where they are unhitched to begin their graceful circling route back to earth. The area is also used by skydivers, many of them tourists who come in from Waikiki. Their descent is much quicker but equally spectacular.

On the way back to Waialua on Farrington Highway, you may find yourself fighting the same steady winds that provided the gliders with lift and the windsurfers with their thrilling rides. The scenery changes again to sugarcane fields until you return to your starting point.

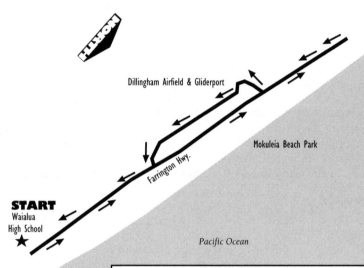

KAENA POINT

NORTH

Dillingham Airfield & Gliderport

Mokuleia Beach Park

Farrington Hwy.

START
Waialua
High School
★

Pacific Ocean

Getting There

Traveling west on the H-1 freeway, take exit 8A to the H-2 freeway. Follow H-2 to where it ends in the outskirts of Wahiawa. H-2 becomes Wilikina Drive, then Kaukonahua Road. Follow Kaukonahua Road downhill where it becomes Farrington Highway. Continue on Farrington Highway until you reach a traffic rotary. Turn left at the rotary to stay on Farrington Highway. Waialua Intermediate and High School will appear on your left after you pass under a cane haul road bridge.

Turned to Stone
Kahuku

Number of miles:	24.2
Approximate pedaling time:	2 hours
Terrain:	Flat
Traffic:	Moderate, but sometimes heavy
Things to see:	Kahuku Sugar Mill, Polynesian Cultural Center, Crouching Lion, Malaekahana State Recreation Area
Food:	Snacks at convenience stores at the Kahuku Sugar Mill and across the street from Swanzy Beach Park
Facilities:	Rest rooms and water at Kahuku Sugar Mill and Swanzy Beach Park

The old sugar mill in Kahuku takes you back to a time when steam power was used to transform green stalks of tropical sugarcane into crystal-white grains of sugar.

Before you start your ride down the windward coast, explore the former sugar mill that now stands quiet, surrounded by a gas station, a busy convenience store, and a few hopeful vendors. Since the mill is virtually intact, you can easily imagine what it must have been like when it was in operation. A self-guided tour is free. The various parts of the mill are color-coded to give an understanding of how the refining process worked.

Huge iron flywheels played an important role in the production of power. Since the steam engines had only one power stroke, the inertia stored in the heavy spinning wheels provided power for the return stroke. The whirling of the huge spoked wheels, the washing and crushing of the cane, and the heating of the extracted fluid must have made for very hot and noisy work.

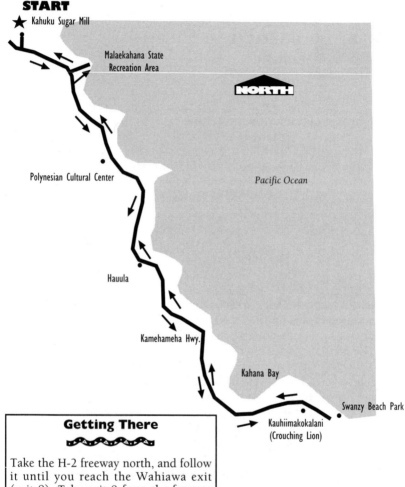

START
★ Kahuku Sugar Mill

Malaekahana State
Recreation Area

NORTH

Polynesian Cultural Center

Pacific Ocean

Hauula

Kamehameha Hwy.

Kahana Bay

Swanzy Beach Park

Kauhiimakokalani
(Crouching Lion)

Getting There

Take the H-2 freeway north, and follow it until you reach the Wahiawa exit (exit 8). Take exit 8 from the freeway onto Kamehameha Highway. Stay on the highway as you pass through Wahiawa town then toward the coast. Continue north passing Sunset Beach and the Turtle Bay Hilton. The Kahuku Sugar Mill will be to the left.

DIREC-TIONS at a glance

0.0	Start the ride at Kahuku Sugar Mill. Turn left onto Kamehameha Highway, and ride south.
11.9	Turn around at Swanzy Beach Park, and retrace your route on Kamehameha Highway.

22.2 Turn right into Malaekahana Bay State Recreation Area.
22.4 Return to Kamehameha Highway.
22.6 Turn right onto Kamehameha Highway.
24.2 Turn right into Kahuku Sugar Mill.

Kahuku, northernmost point on Oahu, stands at one end of the Koolau Range. The hills in Kahuku are small and worn compared with the rest of the range, and the winds sweep over them easily. The primary industry in Kahuku is agriculture, but there is also an experimental windmill farm that produces electricity from the steady winds. As you ride south on Kamehameha Highway, you will likely find yourself fighting these winds. But on the return trip, the same winds will be to your back, making the going much easier.

Between Kahuku and the turnaround point at Swanzy Beach Park, Kamehameha Highway is fairly narrow, and busy with traffic because it's the only road that serves the windward coast. After you ride past the plantation-style cottages in Kahuku, the first point of interest is the Polynesian Cultural Center, on the right side of the road at 3.4 miles. The center is run by the Mormon Church and has model villages of various Pacific island cultures. Daytime tours and evening pageants are available for a fee (808–293–3333).

As you continue down Kamehameha Highway, you will pass through the small coastal town of Hauula, then into Kaliuwaa

Valley. The valley, rich in legend, features a hike to a waterfall popularly known as Sacred Falls.

Farther down the highway, at 11.2 miles into this ride, you'll spot the Crouching Lion. Formed high on top of a cliff, most people see the shape of a lion, but the Hawaiians had a different view of this rock formation. They saw it as Kauhi, a demigod that had been turned to stone. When the goddess Hiiaka passed through the area, Kauhi rose to a crouching position to try to follow her, but he was unable to free himself from the bonds of the rock and has remained there ever since.

Turn around at Swanzy Beach Park, and head back on Kamehameha Highway toward the sugar mill. On the way back, investigate Malaekahana State Recreation Area, which is only about a mile and a half south of the mill. Ride the short access road to a parking area, where you can leave your bike for a quick walk over an embankment and onto a beautiful crescent-shaped beach. The area can be crowded with campers on weekends, but during the week it's usually pleasantly deserted.

High-speed Thrills
Wahiawa and Waialua

Number of miles:	18.2
Approximate pedaling time:	2.5 hours
Terrain:	One high-speed descent, flat sections, and one challenging hill
Traffic:	Light in the mornings, heavier during periods of high surf on the north shore
Things to see:	Wahiawa town, pineapple and sugar-cane fields, Waianae Mountains, Waialua town
Food:	Meals and snacks in Wahiawa, Kemoo Farms, and Dole Pineapple Pavilion
Facilities:	Rest rooms and water at Waialua District Park and Dole Pineapple Plantation

The trade winds are restless in the town of Wahiawa. Swirling across central Oahu and only slightly tamed by the Koolau Mountains, the winds are said to sound like rough seas.

Wahiawa sits on the edge of Schofield Barracks Military Reservation and Wheeler Army Airfield between the Koolau and Waianae Mountains. There was a time when the sugarcane and pineapple fields next to Wahiawa played a major role in Hawaii's economy, but these producers are now struggling. Maybe the noise of the wind is also the sound of change as pineapple and sugarcane growers look to use their land in new ways.

You will definitely get an earful of wind after starting from a row of retail shops at Kemoo Farms near Lake Wilson and riding out of Wahiawa and across the flat, open pineapple fields on Wi-

likina Drive. The wind sweeps over the pineapple as it grows close to the ground in thick, precisely laid ribbons.

Wilikina Drive merges with Kaukonahua Road, which takes you on a high-speed descent from Oahu's central plateau down to sea level into the sleepy plantation town of Waialua. This is one of the most thrilling rides on Oahu. Exercise caution, as the road has no shoulders and twists dramatically in some places.

The price for all the coasting into Waialua is a difficult climb back to Wahiawa. But before you begin the climb, enjoy the flat roads of Waialua that pass by a dirt-stained sugar mill and plantation cottages. Waialua was built around sugarcane production, but these days the mill burns only waste oil and wood scraps, and the town struggles to form a new identity. Waialua District Park appears on your right at 8.1 miles, just as you are exiting town on Goodale Avenue.

On the tough climb out of Waialua and back to the pineapple fields of Wahiawa via Kamehameha Highway, your first inclination is to ask yourself why you are doing it. The wind blows in your face, holding back your momentum, and the road seems full of false summits. As you hunker down against the wind, it feels like the climb will last forever.

But Kamehameha Highway has generous shoulders, giving you ample separation from the passing cars. If you take your time, you can see the beauty in the surroundings. Next to the road, scraps of black plastic sheets laid between rows of pineapple flap in the breeze, and beyond the crops are views of the Waianae Range.

During the climb it is reassuring to know there is a reward waiting at the top of the hill. Dole Pineapple Pavilion is located on the left-hand side of Kamehameha Highway at a point 15.5 miles into your day's ride. Cyclists who conquer the climb have earned the pineapple whips and other treats available at the pavilion.

Later, as you bear right onto Kamananui Road, stop to explore the pineapple variety garden located on the left. It's a good chance to inspect the many varieties of pineapples up close as they grow between thick thorny spines.

Goodale Ave.

WAIALUA

Goodale Ave.

Waialua Beach Rd.

Waialua District Park

Kealohanui St.

Traffic Circle

Kamehameha Hwy.

NORTH

Farrington Hwy.

Dole Pineapple Pavillion

Kaukonahua Rd.

Pineapple Variety Garden

Kamanaui Rd.

Wilikina Dr.

★ **START**
Kemoo Farms

Schofield Barracks

Getting There

Heading west on the H-1 freeway, take exit 8A and travel north on the H-2 freeway. Wahiawa is located in the center of Oahu, at the end of the H-2 freeway.

DIREC-TIONS at a glance

0.0 Start the ride on Wilikina Drive next to Kemoo Farms and head north.

2.5 Wilikina Drive merges onto Kaukonahua Road, which later becomes Farrington Highway.

7.4 Turn right from Farrington Highway onto Goodale Avenue.

7.9 Turn left onto Kealohanui Street.

7.95 Turn right onto Goodale Avenue.

8.2 Turn right onto Waialua Beach Road.

9.3 Turn right entering the traffic circle; follow signs for Wahiawa.

9.6 Turn right onto Kamehameha Highway.

16.3 Bear right onto Kamananui Road.

17.5 Turn left onto Wilikina Drive.

18.2 Turn right into Schofield Barracks; make a U-turn, and use the same traffic light to make a left onto Wilikina Drive to return to Kemoo Farms.

The North Shore
Haleiwa to Sunset Beach

Number of miles:	15.2
Approximate pedaling time:	2 hours
Terrain:	Mostly flat
Traffic:	Moderate; heavier during periods of high surf
Things to see:	Waimea Falls Park, Sunset Beach, Ehukai Beach Park, Waimea Bay Beach Park, historic town of Haleiwa
Food:	Meals and snacks in Haleiwa
Facilities:	Rest rooms and water at North Shore Market Place

During the winter, the north shore of Oahu is assaulted by huge ocean swells generated by storms in the North Pacific. Professional wave riders from all over the world come to risk their lives in competitions held when the waves are at their height.

Before it became the surfing capital of the Pacific, Haleiwa was dominated by sugar growers, and it still retains the flavor of a small plantation town. The historic wooden buildings along the road are inviting. But these days, instead of finding a blacksmith or a general store, you are more likely to find bikini shops and cafes.

Start your ride from the North Shore Market Place. Turn right onto Kamehameha Highway and continue through town. Riding the narrow bridge over the Anahulu River takes you out of Haleiwa and on your way to Oahu's premier surfing areas. In the past, the bridge was a bottleneck during periods of heavy surf. People would drive in from all over the island, and huge traffic

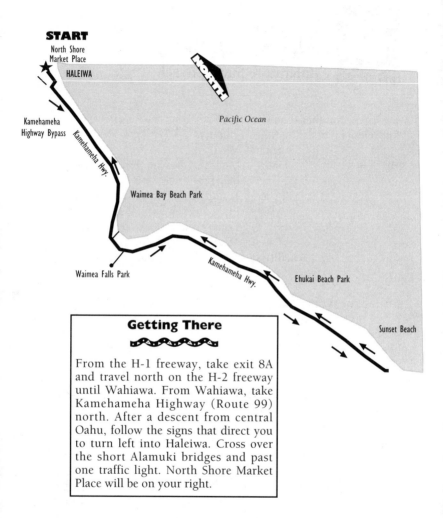

START
North Shore
Market Place
HALEIWA

NORTH

Kamehameha
Highway Bypass

Kamehameha Hwy.

Pacific Ocean

Waimea Bay Beach Park

Waimea Falls Park

Kamehameha Hwy.

Ehukai Beach Park

Sunset Beach

Getting There

From the H-1 freeway, take exit 8A
and travel north on the H-2 freeway
until Wahiawa. From Wahiawa, take
Kamehameha Highway (Route 99)
north. After a descent from central
Oahu, follow the signs that direct you
to turn left into Haleiwa. Cross over
the short Alamuki bridges and past
one traffic light. North Shore Market
Place will be on your right.

DIREC-TIONS at a glance

0.0	Turn right from the North Shore Market Place onto Kamehameha Highway.
1.1	Turn left at the traffic light, staying on Kamehameha Highway.
7.6	Turn around at Sunset Beach. Retrace your route back toward Haleiwa (or use the bike path that runs roughly parallel to the road).
14.0	Turn right, staying on Kamehameha Highway.
15.2	Turn left into the North Shore Market Place.

jams would develop. Since construction of the Kamehameha Highway bypass, Haleiwa is considerably less congested.

Beyond Haleiwa, Kamehameha Highway is fairly straight and narrow. Farms and tall grass dot the landscape until you reach Waimea Valley at 4.6 miles. The road dips down, crosses a bridge, and then on the right-hand side is Waimea Falls Park. The park charges an entry fee and features a hike to the falls. You can also take part in Hawaiian activities like ulu maika, a game similar to bowling.

Continue on Kamehameha Highway from Waimea Valley until the Sunset Beach turnaround point.

When a big winter swell arrives at Sunset Beach, it is truly exciting to watch. You can see the waves as they transform from gentle ripples into huge sharp-peaked walls of water. As the waves break, the tips are blown into a spray that forms a salty haze over the entire coast. Even professional surfers with many years of experience are wary of the north shore's mighty 25-foot waves. If the thundering crunch of the waves does not scare you, the venomous hiss of foam washing high on the beach probably will.

From Sunset Beach, you can return to Haleiwa on the same route you took riding out. You may also use the bike path that runs roughly parallel to the road. Although the path is usually crowded with people carrying surfboards and extends only to Waimea, it still provides more intimate views of famous surfing spots, like Banzai Pipeline at Ehukai Beach Park.

Also on the return trip, visit Waimea Bay Beach Park, across the highway from Waimea Falls Park. It's equally beautiful, and it's free of charge. Past the park, pull off the highway as you are climbing out of the valley, and look back for a panoramic view of Waimea Bay.

The wind normally blows favorably on the return trip. Before you know it, you will find yourself back in Haleiwa, relaxing and perhaps sipping an iced coffee.

Passing Near Moist Blackness
Waimanalo

Number of miles:	22.2
Approximate pedaling time:	2.5 hours
Terrain:	A few hills, mostly flat
Traffic:	Heavy on Kalanianaole Highway, light on the back roads of Waimanalo
Things to see:	Sea Life Park, Koolau Mountains, farms and beaches in Waimanalo
Food:	Snacks at convenience stores in Waimanalo
Facilities:	Rest rooms at Maunawili Park and Makapuu Beach Park

The Koolau Range is the most spectacular feature of Oahu's windward coast, and nowhere can you get a more intimate view of these mountains than from Waimanalo.

Start your ride at Maunawili Elementary School, located next to Maunawili Park, and travel south on Kalanianaole Highway. Take a brief detour onto Old Kalanianaole Road, a peaceful route that takes you through an upscale neighborhood under the shadow of Olomana Peak.

Back on the highway, you will enjoy a nice downhill run into Waimanalo, primarily an agricultural area. The University of Hawaii has an experimental farm there. Privately owned farms produce bananas, papayas, corn, and a variety of other crops.

Detour again from the highway to explore the back roads of Waimanalo. You will know you are in the country when you make the left turn onto Waikupanaha Street and smell the unmistakable odor of a nearby pig farm. The Koolaus behind Waimanalo present sheer cliffs more than 2,000 feet high. In the

early-morning sunshine, the cliffs take on an emerald hue as they stand covered in a velvet cloak of green. Beyond Waimanalo, as you head toward Makapuu Beach Park, the mountains begin to look blue-gray as they become less covered with vegetation, and bare rock begins to show through.

After you return to Kalanianaole Highway, you will see Manana Island off the coast of Makapuu on your left. Also called Rabbit Island, this extinct volcano stands some 200 feet above sea level and serves as a seabird sanctuary. Sea Life Park will appear on your right, just before Makapuu Beach Park, and for a fee you can tour exhibits that include green sea turtles, endangered Hawaiian monk seals, and performing dolphins.

Turn around at the beach park and take Kalanianaole Highway back to Waimanalo. The highway follows close to the beach, and the perfect weather will tempt you to get off your bike for a barefoot walk on the sand. In the distance the forked hill of Olomana shows prominently. The sharp peak, standing 1,643 feet tall, was named for a giant who landed there after jumping from the island of Kauai.

Kalanianaole Highway is busy through downtown Waimanalo, so ride with caution. Your next obstacle is climbing the Waimanalo ridge as you are leaving town. Once at the top, however, you can rest on the flats until you turn onto Keolu Drive for a high-speed descent.

Keolu Drive drops into the area called Enchanted Lake, looping through a residential area and circling around the lake. But don't be surprised if you never see water. Once used as a fishing pond, the lake is easy to miss because it's small and obscured by grass, fences, and houses. The Hawaiian name for the pond is Kaelepulu, or "moist blackness."

Climbing out of Enchanted Lake on Keolu Drive is hardly enchanting at all. The road is steep, and there is a fair amount of traffic. Worst of all, there is no satisfying descent once you reach the top and turn right onto Kalanianaole Highway. Thankfully, the road is smooth and eventually you do get a small descent just before you return to Maunawili Elementary School.

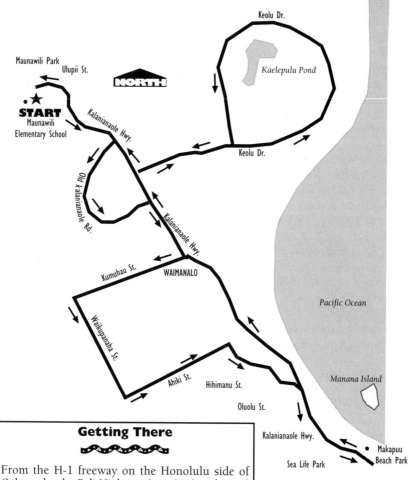

Maunawili Park
Ulupii St.
START
Maunawili Elementary School

Kalanianaole Hwy.

Old Kalanianaole Rd.

Kalanianaole Hwy.

NORTH

Keolu Dr.

Kaelepulu Pond

Keolu Dr.

Kumuhau St.

WAIMANALO

Waikupanaha St.

Ahiki St.

Hihimanu St.

Oluolu St.

Pacific Ocean

Manana Island

Kalanianaole Hwy.

Sea Life Park

Makapuu
Beach Park

Getting There

From the H-1 freeway on the Honolulu side of Oahu, take the Pali Highway (exit 21B) and travel north over the Koolau Mountain Range. Once through the Pali Tunnels, continue on Pali Highway, which later becomes Kalanianaole Highway. Pass through three traffic signals, and turn right at the fourth one, staying on Kalanianaole Highway. From the highway take your second right onto Ulupii Street. Maunawili Elementary School and Maunawili Park will be to the left.

DIREC-TIONS at a glance

0.0 Start the ride from Maunawili Elementary School.

0.1 Turn right from Ulupii Street onto Kalanianaole Highway.

0.5 Turn right from Kalanianaole Highway onto Old Kalanianaole Road.

2.2 Turn right back onto Kalanianaole Highway and ride into Waimanalo.

3.1 Turn right onto Kumuhau Street.

4.1 Turn left onto Waikupanaha Street.

5.8 Turn left onto Ahiki Street.

6.5 Turn right onto Hihimanu Street.

7.3 Turn right onto Oluolu Street.

7.8 Turn right onto Kalanianaole Highway.

14.7 Turn left into Makapuu Beach Park. Turn around at the park, and ride Kalanianaole Highway back to Waimanalo.

16.9 Turn right onto Keolu Drive.

20.8 Turn right again onto Keolu Drive.

21.0 Turn right onto Kalanianaole Highway.

22.1 Turn left onto Ulupii Street.

22.2 Return to Maunawili Elementary School.

14 Lizard Island
Kaneohe to Mokolii

Number of miles:	18.2
Approximate pedaling time:	2 hours
Terrain:	One hill, otherwise mostly flat
Traffic:	Moderately busy first 4 miles, busy the rest of the way
Things to see:	Heeia State Park, Kualoa Regional Park, Mokolii Island, Koolau Mountains
Food:	Meals and snacks at Kaneohe Bay Shopping Center and Windward Mall
Facilities:	Rest rooms at Windward Mall and Kualoa Regional Park

Few features on the windward coast of Oahu stir the imagination like the tiny island of Mokolii. Geologists might give you a lecture about ancient volcanic eruptions and the fantastic eroding powers of the sea. But many folks are just as happy to think of the island as a Chinaman's hat, a poi pounder, the tail of a giant lizard, or a shark's fin. Whatever your personal theory, the ride to Kualoa Regional Park is fun and provides a close view of the island.

Start from the Kaneohe Bay Shopping Center and ride north on Kamehameha Highway. For the next 4 miles, the highway is narrow but relatively uncrowded. You will pass houses and then cross a long, narrow bridge over Heeia stream. To the right of the bridge, Heeia Pond has been taken over by an impenetrable stand of mangrove, an introduced plant that has destroyed many native habitats.

Heeia is said to be the place where souls were judged and the place where a tidal wave once helped ancient Hawaiians defeat an opposing force from leeward Oahu. Heeia State Park is at the top of a brief climb, at 1.4 miles from the start of the ride, and beyond the park the highway flattens and follows the coast. If the weather is good, the first sight of Mokolii from the road comes at 3.1 miles. In the distance, the island urges you to get closer as it sits quietly on smooth water.

Kahekili Highway joins Kamehameha Highway at 4.1 miles, adding more traffic to the narrow roadway. Continue riding on Kamehameha Highway past the valleys of Waihole and Waikane. Both valleys, situated in the heart of the windward coast where rainfall is abundant, are heavily vegetated. The warm climate and the rainfall make the area ideal for growing taro, the plant used to make poi. Some of the valleys' water is diverted through the Koolau Mountains to the dry sections of central Oahu, though windward farmers have begun challenging this practice.

The jungle and tall trees of parts of Waikane Valley hide un-exploded ordnance. In the past, the military used the valley for target practice, and the remaining live ordnance makes half the valley unusable.

As you approach Kualoa Regional Park, you will encounter a few rolling hills, but these are easily forgotten when you turn into the park and see Mokolii up close. One legend about Mokolii begins on the Big Island, where Pele, the volcano goddess, sends her sister, Hiiaka, on a mission to Kauai. On her journey, Hiiaka encounters an evil creature near Kualoa. The creature was a moo (pronounced MO-oh), similar to a dragon or huge lizard. Hiiaka kills the moo, and its tail is the island you see today. In Hawaiian, Mokolii means "little moo."

On the return ride to Kaneohe, be wary of a curb that is built into the roadway before you reach Kahaluu and the junction of Kahekili and Kamehameha Highways. The curb runs for less than a mile, but it makes the road narrow and prevents you from riding on the shoulder. This condition exists only in the south-bound direction of Kamehameha Highway. On Kahekili Highway, after Temple Valley, a deep gulch presents the toughest

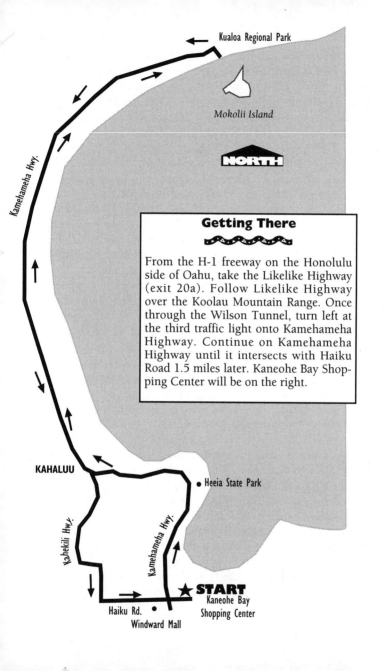

← Kualoa Regional Park

Mokolii Island

NORTH

Kamehameha Hwy.

Getting There

From the H-1 freeway on the Honolulu side of Oahu, take the Likelike Highway (exit 20a). Follow Likelike Highway over the Koolau Mountain Range. Once through the Wilson Tunnel, turn left at the third traffic light onto Kamehameha Highway. Continue on Kamehameha Highway until it intersects with Haiku Road 1.5 miles later. Kaneohe Bay Shopping Center will be on the right.

KAHALUU

• Heeia State Park

Kahekili Hwy.

Kamehameha Hwy.

★ **START**
Kaneohe Bay
Shopping Center

Haiku Rd. •
Windward Mall

DIREC-TIONS at a glance

0.0 From Kaneohe Bay Shopping Center, ride north on Kamehameha Highway.

4.1 Turn right, staying on Kamehameha Highway.

9.0 Turn right into Kualoa Regional Park.

9.2 Turn around at the parking area. Return to Kamehameha Highway.

9.4 Turn left onto Kamehameha Highway and ride back toward Kaneohe.

13.6 The road narrows due to hazardous curb. This curb only exists in the southbound direction of Kamehameha Highway. Ride with caution.

14.3 The road widens after the bridge in Kahaluu. Continue straight from Kamehameha Highway onto Kahekili Highway.

17.5 Turn left onto Haiku Road.

18.2 Return to Kaneohe Bay Shopping Center.

uphill challenge of the day. Here, however, the shoulder is wider, and you can take the hill at your own speed. Once past the gulch, turn left on Haiku Road and pass Windward Mall on your right before returning to Kaneohe Bay Shopping Center.

Makakilo Stomp
Kapolei

Number of miles:	8.1
Approximate pedaling time:	1.5 hours
Terrain:	One steep hill 2.5 miles long, otherwise flat
Traffic:	Lightest in the morning
Things to see:	Kapolei, Mauna Kapu, views of south Oahu
Food:	Meals and snacks at Kapolei Shopping Center
Facilities:	Rest rooms at Kapolei Community Park

Charging up a hill is the best way to stretch your legs and get your heart pounding. Makakilo Drive, on the Ewa end of the Waianae Range, presents such an opportunity with a hill 2.5 miles long.

This ride begins at Kapolei Community Park, and before you start your climb, warm up by exploring Kapolei, a new planned community. Starting a city from scratch has allowed the planners to get a lot of things right. Besides underground utilities that free the skies of telephone poles and tangles of wires, Kapolei has wide streets and smooth bike lanes. In most places, parking on the street is forbidden, which eliminates the fear of crashing into an open car door. To top it off, the shopping areas even have bicycle racks.

You'll find a great view of Mauna Kapu in the Waianae Mountains from Kamaaha Loop. Thoughtful height restrictions on buildings play an important role in keeping the mountains in view. Rising well over 2,000 feet, Mauna Kapu is the mountain

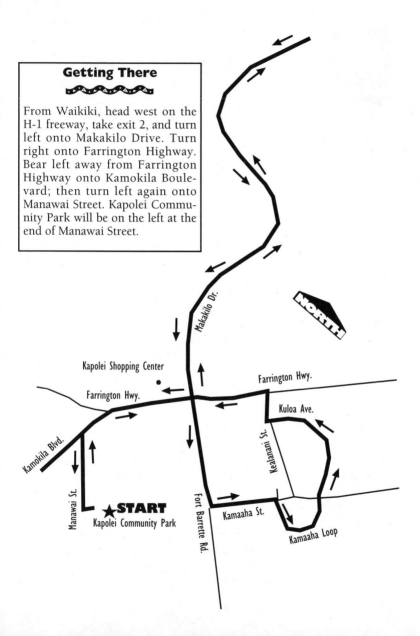

Getting There

From Waikiki, head west on the H-1 freeway, take exit 2, and turn left onto Makakilo Drive. Turn right onto Farrington Highway. Bear left away from Farrington Highway onto Kamokila Boulevard; then turn left again onto Manawai Street. Kapolei Community Park will be on the left at the end of Manawai Street.

NORTH

Makakilo Dr.

Kapolei Shopping Center

Farrington Hwy.

Farrington Hwy.

Kuloa Ave.

Kealanani St.

Kamokila Blvd.

Manawai St.

★START
Kapolei Community Park

Fort Barrette Rd.

Kamaaha St.

Kamaaha Loop

DIREC-TIONS at a glance

0.0 From Kapolei Community Park, turn right onto Manawai Street.

0.1 Turn right onto Kamokila Boulevard, which becomes Farrington Highway.

0.6 Turn right onto Fort Barrette Road.

1.1 Turn left onto Kamaaha Street.

1.4 Turn right onto Kamaaha Loop.

1.7 After stopping at the sign, proceed straight across the intersection onto Kuloa Avenue.

2.2 Turn right onto Kealanani Street.

2.4 Turn left onto Farrington Highway.

2.6 Turn right onto Makakilo Drive.

5.1 Turn around at the top of the hill and retrace your route back down the hill.

7.6 Turn right onto Farrington Highway.

7.9 Veer left onto Kamokila Boulevard.

8.0 Turn left onto Manawai Street

8.1 Turn left into Kapolei Community Park.

you will soon be riding on. Its slopes look gentle and are covered with a light green grass that turns golden brown during the summer.

The climate in Makakilo and Kapolei is arid because the prevailing winds flow over the Koolau Mountains before reaching this area. Over the Koolaus, the air loses its moisture in the form of rain and has little left for leeward Oahu. Many times, when it's raining elsewhere on the island, you can count on Kapolei and Makakilo to be dry and hot.

After you turn onto Makakilo Drive, the beginning of this climb is all business. In no time at all you will look down and realize you are already in your easiest gear. The road is wide and smooth, but the grade is unrelenting. Along the road, homes are built on the slopes of the mountain. Sadly, there are no designated viewpoints along the roadway, so you have to make the most of views between the houses. The views that are possible, however, are spectacular as you look down the mountain and across the Ewa plain to Honolulu and Diamond Head.

As you near the top, Makakilo Drive finally levels off. A private road continues even farther up the mountain, almost to the very top of Mauna Kapu, but it's rarely, if ever, open to the public. Turn around and retrace your route down the hill. The wind will roar in your ears as you plummet down to Farrington Highway, where you turn right to head back to Kapolei Community Park.

Roller Coaster
Waimea Canyon Loop

Number of miles:	25.1
Approximate pedaling time:	4 hours
Terrain:	Challenging hill
Traffic:	Light
Things to see:	Waimea Canyon
Food:	Meals and snacks in Waimea
Facilities:	Water and rest rooms at Waimea Athletic Field, rest rooms at the canyon lookout

The weathering forces of nature created Waimea Canyon, a huge gash that cuts deep into Kauai. The canyon is a masterpiece of erosional sculpting.

If you complete this ride, you will have the satisfaction of knowing that you conquered one of Hawaii's most difficult rides. The climb to the rim of the canyon is almost 12 miles long, and it's tough even for experienced riders. The rewards are great, however, with spectacular scenery and a roller-coaster descent that will make you want to do it again as soon as you reach the bottom.

Start the ride in the town of Waimea, and warm up your climbing legs by pedaling the smooth highway to the neighboring coastal community of Kekaha. You will soon be past the Kekaha sugar mill and on Kokee Road, where the climb begins.

The sunshine is intense on the west side of Kauai, and the landscape is characterized by a flat coastal plain with sharp sloping mountains directly behind. The mountains' wide ridges extend up to the rim of Waimea Canyon. Sugarcane is cultivated in the rich soil of these ridges, which are separated by steep, dry gullies thorny with weeds.

At the beginning of the climb, Kokee Road is narrow, with a few rough sections. The road meanders up through the gullies, then steepens at a point 6 miles into the ride, where it ascends to the top of a ridge. Peer into one of the eroded gullies, and you'll see drops of more than 100 feet—plenty of incentive to stay on the pavement. As you look down from the ridge, green fields of sugarcane give way to the coast below. Beyond the coast, the sparkling quartz-blue ocean meets the sky and spreads across the horizon.

As you approach the canyon rim, you leave the cane fields behind and enter Waimea Canyon State Park. Trees now dot the roadside, and a combination of cloud cover and higher altitude creates a cooler climate. After turning left onto Waimea Canyon Drive, there are only two difficult sections ahead. Thankfully, a brief downhill leg between these sections allows your tired legs to recover.

The access road to the lookout finally arrives, bringing you to the top. Once you take in the view, you will realize that every pedal stroke was worth it. On the 3,000-foot cliffs of the canyon, layers of long-ago lava flows are clearly defined, painting the walls in multiple colors. Clouds keep changing the appearance of the canyon as they cast fantastic shadows that move across the cliffs and the valley floor. Across the canyon, you can see waterfalls doing their work that has been going on for many centuries. The waterfalls are sometimes blown by the wind, and instead of falling straight down, the water sprays off to the side in a curtain of mist that floats softly to the ground.

Now that you're at the top, it's time to be repaid for all your hard work with a joyous ride down Waimea Canyon Drive, a steep run that feels almost like skydiving. Soon after the 18-mile mark of your day's trip, Waimea Canyon Drive dips and turns like a roller coaster. If you let go of the brakes for a few seconds, you will suddenly find yourself approaching a speed of 40 miles an hour.

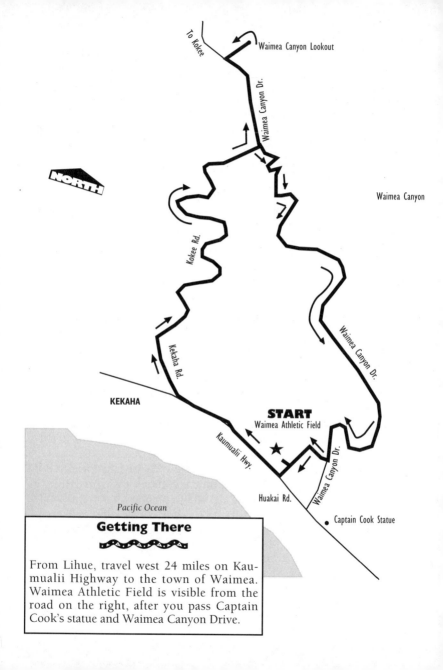

To Kokee

Waimea Canyon Lookout

Waimea Canyon Dr.

Waimea Canyon

NORTH

Kokee Rd.

Kekaha Rd.

Waimea Canyon Dr.

KEKAHA

START
Waimea Athletic Field

Kaumualii Hwy.

Waimea Canyon Dr.

Huakai Rd.

Captain Cook Statue

Pacific Ocean

Getting There

From Lihue, travel west 24 miles on Kau-mualii Highway to the town of Waimea. Waimea Athletic Field is visible from the road on the right, after you pass Captain Cook's statue and Waimea Canyon Drive.

**DIREC-
TIONS
at a glance**

0.0 From the Waimea Athletic Field on Huakai Road, turn right onto Kaumualii Highway, and ride west.

1.3 Turn right onto Kekaha Road.

2.6 Turn right onto Kokee Road.

10.4 Bear left onto Waimea Canyon Drive.

14.1 Turn right onto the access road for the Waimea Canyon Lookout.

14.3 Turn around at the Waimea Canyon Lookout and leave the way you came in.

14.5 Turn left onto Waimea Canyon Drive.

18.1 Bear left to stay on Waimea Canyon Drive.

24.8 Turn right onto Huakai Road.

24.9 After stopping at the sign, turn left, staying on Huakai Road.

25.1 Turn right into the Waimea Athletic Field.

Waimea Canyon Drive follows close to the rim of the canyon, so there are buffeting winds and grave consequences for going off the road. Exercise extreme caution, and do not allow yourself to pick up more speed than you can handle down this wicked descent.

Once at the bottom, and back in Waimea, it's hard to restrain a cheer. This exciting trip is what bike riding is all about.

Fine Island Ride
Kapaa to Kilauea Point

Number of miles:	34.0
Approximate pedaling time:	4 hours
Terrain:	Rolling hills
Traffic:	Light
Things to see:	Kilauea Point National Wildlife Refuge, Mokuaeae Island, missionary church
Food:	Meals and snacks in Kapaa
Facilities:	Water and rest rooms at Kapaa Beach Park and Kilauea Point National Wildlife Refuge

If you enjoy bird watching, grab your binoculars and take a ride out to Kilauea Point National Wildlife Refuge.

The ride starts from Kapaa, a busy little town on the east shore of Kauai. This town has something for everyone, whether you like relaxing at the beach or kayaking up the Wailua River. But save these activities for after your ride to the wildlife refuge, which is open daily from 10 A.M. to 4 P.M.

Your route to and from Kilauea Point, on Kuhio Highway, takes you over a series of rolling hills. The pavement is smooth, with shoulders the whole way, though they vary in width. On most of the uphill sections, the shoulders are wide enough to keep you a safe distance from passing cars. The steepest sections come as you pass through the Anahola Bay area, about 6 miles from Kapaa.

Northeastern Kauai greets the prevailing trade winds first and enjoys more rainfall than west Kauai, with grass and shrubs

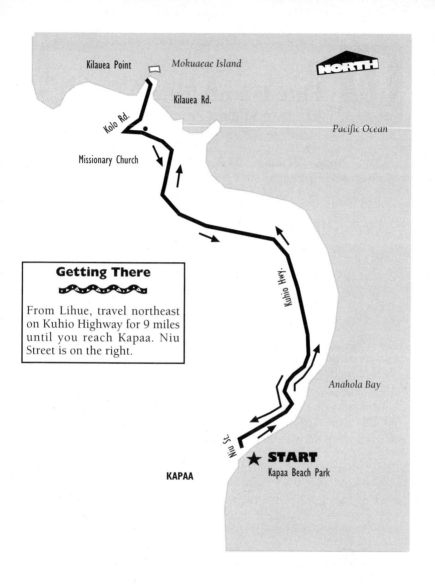

Kilauea Point

Mokuaeae Island

NORTH

Kilauea Rd.

Kolo Rd.

Pacific Ocean

Missionary Church

Kuhio Hwy.

Getting There

From Lihue, travel northeast on Kuhio Highway for 9 miles until you reach Kapaa. Niu Street is on the right.

Anahola Bay

Niu St.

★ **START**
Kapaa Beach Park

KAPAA

DIREC-TIONS at a glance

0.0	Start at Kapaa Beach Park at the end of Niu Street, and ride toward Kuhio Highway.
0.1	Turn right onto Kuhio Highway.
15.3	Turn right onto Kolo Road.
15.4	Turn left onto Kilauea Road.
17.0	Turn around at the Kilauea Point National Wildlife Refuge and retrace your route on Kilauea Road.
18.7	Turn right onto Kolo Road.
18.8	Turn left onto Kuhio Highway.
33.9	Turn left onto Niu Street.
34.0	Return to Kapaa Beach Park.

keeping the countryside green. Looking toward the interior of the island, you will see the Anahola and Makaleha Mountains. Behind these mountains, in the center of Kauai, is the peak of Mount Waialeale. Rising more than 5,000 feet high, the mountains of central Kauai are often covered in clouds because they receive more rain than any other place on earth. An average of 444 inches of rain a year falls on Mount Waialeale.

When you finally turn off Kuhio Highway and enter Kilauea, you still have to ride another 2 miles and down a steep driveway before the coast comes into view at Kilauea Point National Wildlife Refuge. The refuge does not charge a fee, but a donation is requested at the visitor center.

At the refuge, get off your bike and walk to the viewpoint perched on top of a huge sea cliff. Directly below the cliff you will see the small island of Mokuaeae. When the blue ocean swells meet this jagged island, they explode into foam, creating a snowy white ring around the black rocky coast.

The main attraction at the refuge is the sight of hundreds of

83

seabirds. With a good pair of binoculars, you can track red-footed boobies, great frigate birds, and tropic birds as they float effortlessly on the trade winds or nest in nearby cliffs. The refuge also protects endangered species such as the Hawaiian goose (the nene) and the Hawaiian monk seal. On rare occasions, you may even see green sea turtles or whales.

A well-preserved lighthouse stands prominently at the edge of the refuge lookout. This lighthouse is no longer in service, its duties now handled by a smaller light station hidden in front of the old one.

After leaving the refuge, check out the small church on your left as you turn back onto Kolo Road. The stone church, a lasting reminder of the Christian missionaries who came to Hawaii in the 1800s, features beautifully crafted stained-glass windows and a small graveyard with lava rock headstones.

If you're lucky on the return trip, you will benefit from a tailwind that whisks you back into town from the outskirts of Kapaa.

First Contact
West Kauai

Number of miles:	32.3
Approximate pedaling time:	3 hours
Terrain:	Low rolling hills, mostly flat
Traffic:	Light
Things to see:	Coastal towns of Waimea and Kekaha, island of Niihau, statue of Captain Cook, a Russian fort, fields of sugarcane
Food:	Snacks in Hanapepe and Waimea
Facilities:	Rest rooms and water at Hanapepe, Waimea, and the Russian fort

If you like to ride on smooth roads and want to feel the warmth of the sun on your back, set your sights on the west side of Kauai.

Starting from the stadium in Hanapepe, ride west on Kaumualii Highway. After climbing a short hill that takes you out of town, you will find yourself on smooth roadway lined with sugarcane fields. Once a viable crop on all the main islands, sugarcane is now grown only on Kauai and Maui. Kaumualii Highway continues between the cane fields and over low rolling hills to the town of Waimea.

For Hawaii, Waimea was the site of first contact with the West. It was the landing place in 1778 of Captain Cook, the first explorer from the West to document the existence of the Hawaiian Islands. Cook restocked his ships on Kauai before heading off to explore the North Pacific. He returned to the islands a year later and was killed in a scuffle at Kealakekua Bay on the Big Is-

land. The reports that were brought back to England by Cook's crew enticed more Westerners, and their influences, to the islands. As you ride though the center of Waimea, look for the statue of Captain Cook on your right.

Beyond Waimea you will enter a flat area called the Mana Plain. This geological feature was formed as sand and sedimentary debris built up above sea level. Behind Waimea and its neighboring town of Kekaha, you can see mountains that were formerly sea cliffs.

Kekaha is a quiet town unspoiled by crowds and huge resorts. All the elements of nature combine to make the beaches in Kekaha beautiful. On clear days you can make out the blue-gray outline in the distance of Niihau, an island that supports a small Hawaiian-speaking community. Few people have ever been to the island because it's privately owned, and visits are by invitation only.

Beyond Kekaha on Kaumualii Highway is the military's Pacific Missile Range Facility. On the way to the military facility, heat from the land makes the roadway in the distance glimmer as if it's made of molten glass. Make sure you have plenty of sunscreen and water as this part of Kauai is beastly hot. Thankfully, it's possible to ride quickly because the terrain is flat and the road is wonderfully smooth.

When you reach the main gate of the facility, you'll discover there isn't much to see. You would expect a missile range that boasts 42,000 square miles of controlled airspace and nearly 1,000 square miles of underwater territory to be more impressive, but all you can see beyond the fence is a missile on display, a few buildings, a control tower, and a communications dish.

On the return trip to Kekaha, you may experience a tailwind from the trade winds that sometimes wrap around the central mountains of Kauai. Expect this effect to diminish, however, as you travel farther east.

Along the way, investigate the old Russian fort just east of Waimea. Beneath the brush that now obscures the fort, you will find what was once a formidable structure of rock. Take a few

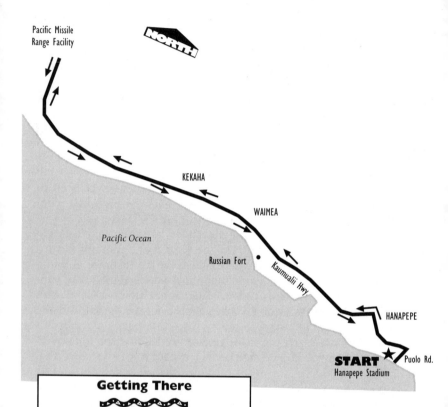

Pacific Missile
Range Facility

NORTH

KEKAHA

WAIMEA

Pacific Ocean

Russian Fort

Kaumualii Hwy

HANAPEPE

START
Hanapepe Stadium

Puolo Rd.

Getting There

From Lihue, travel 18 miles west on
Kaumualii Highway. Past the Hanapepe
McDonald's. Stay on Kaumualii Highway until you see Puolu Road. Turn left
on Puolo Road, and the stadium will be
to your right.

DIREC-TIONS at a glance

0.0 Start at the Hanapepe Stadium, on Puolo Road, and ride to Kaumualii Highway.

0.1 Turn left onto Kaumualii Highway.

16.1 Turn around at the Pacific Missile Range Facility and retrace your route back to Hanapepe.

32.2 Turn right onto Puolo Road.

32.3 Return to Hanapepe Stadium.

minutes to walk inside and to read the plaque that outlines the fort's history.

There are two gradual inclines along the rest of the route to your starting point. Neither incline is difficult if it's not too windy, and you will soon find yourself descending back into Hanapepe.

Wandering Poipu
South Kauai

Number of miles:	12.3
Approximate pedaling time:	1.5 hours
Terrain:	Mostly flat
Traffic:	Light
Things to see:	Old sugar mill, Spouting Horn, Poipu Beach
Food:	Meals and snacks in Koloa and Poipu Shopping Village
Facilities:	Water and rest rooms at Koloa, Spouting Horn, and Poipu Beach

Riding to Poipu allows you to peer into Hawaii's past, and it gives you a glimpse into Hawaii's future.

First explore Hawaii's history by riding into the town of Koloa, where you can see the ruins of an old sugar mill and visit the Sugar Mill Memorial. The memorial is dedicated to the Hawaiian, Portuguese, Chinese, Japanese, Korean, and Filipino workers who toiled in the fields to make Hawaii one of the world's leading producers of sugar.

The first sugarcane fields appeared in Koloa in 1835, when William Hooper started planting cane. Once it became clear that sugarcane was profitable, Hawaii changed dramatically as sugar plantations appeared on all the major islands and large numbers of foreign workers were imported. Eventually the few individuals who came to profit from the production of sugar gained enough power to overthrow the monarchy. The repercussions of this illegal act are still being felt today as lawmakers struggle to find a way to compensate the Hawaiians.

With the sugar industry in decline, Kauai is staking its future on tourism. A mild climate and abundant sunshine make the Koloa area perfect for attracting tourists. On Lawai Road, during this ride, you will find vacation cottages and low-rise condominiums perched next to the rocky coastline.

Lawai Road provides a smooth, flat ride to the Spouting Horn, a natural hole in the rocks next to the sea. At the lookout, wait for a big wave to hit the shore, and watch as water is forced through the hole and shoots into the sky. The spray is accompanied by an eerie whooshing noise that sounds like a whale or an animal trapped in the rocks.

On the way to the Spouting Horn, keep an eye out on your right for a small park with stone terraces and ti plants. The park is a memorial to Prince Jonah Kuhio Kalanianaole, a former delegate to Congress who worked to provide homes for Hawaiians by creating the Hawaiian Homes Commission Act.

From the Spouting Horn, retrace your route on Lawai Road, and then explore the area around Poipu Beach. Here you will find resorts next to the shore, but unlike Waikiki, they are small, low, and spread out. The beaches of Poipu are in protective coves nestled between sections of rocky coastline. Crowds congregate at these small beaches to suntan and swim. Hoone Road, narrow but relatively free of heavy traffic, takes you past Poipu Beach and up a brief hill, where it connects with Pee Road (pronounced PAY-ay).

Pee Road has speed bumps. It eventually leads you inland, away from the coastal resorts. On Weliweli Road you will travel uphill on a gentle grade back to Koloa town. To your right you will see the volcanic crater known as Puu Wanawana, which is covered in weeds and shrubs. Hidden behind this crater is Puu Hunihuni, where the last eruption on Kauai took place.

Farther along Weliweli Road is a modern sugar mill, and beyond that, the towering mountains of Haupu Ridge. At its highest point, the ridge is more than 2,000 feet high and forms a formidable barrier between Poipu and Lihue.

Once back in Koloa, use Wailaau Road to return to Anne Knudsen Park. Wailaau Road takes you through a quiet residen-

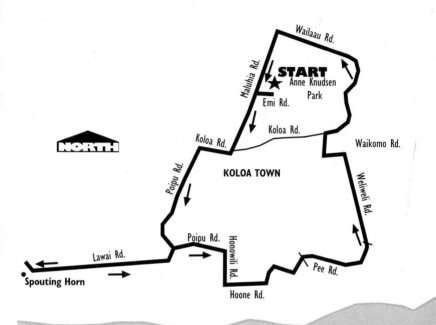

Getting There

From Lihue, drive 7 miles west on Kaumualii Highway, then turn left onto Maluhia Road. Follow Maluhia Road past the tunnel of trees until you reach Anne Knudsen Park, located on the left just outside of Koloa town.

0.0 From Anne Knudsen Park on Emi Road, turn left onto Maluhia Road.

0.3 Turn right onto Koloa Road.

0.4 Turn left onto Poipu Road.

1.9 Turn right onto Lawai Road.

3.8 Turn around at the Spouting Horn, and retrace your route on Lawai Road.

5.9 Turn right onto Poipu Road.

7.0 Turn right onto Honowili Road.

7.2 Turn left onto Hoone Road.

8.1 Hoone Road becomes Pee Road.

8.7 After the stop sign, proceed straight through the intersection onto Weliweli Road.

10.6 After the stop sign, turn left, staying on Weliweli Road.

11.0 Turn right onto Waikomo Road.

11.2 Turn right onto Koloa Road, which becomes Wailaau Road.

12.1 Turn left onto Maluhia Road.

12.3 Turn left onto Emi Road and return to Anne Knudsen Park.

tial neighborhood that is modest in comparison with the resorts only a few miles away. The exception is the house you will encounter on your right that has two huge Easter Island statues and other Polynesian figures in the front yard.

Lanai Special
Shipwreck Beach

Number of miles:	24.4
Approximate pedaling time:	3 hours
Terrain:	Hills
Traffic:	Light
Things to see:	Lanai City, Lodge at Koele, Shipwreck Beach
Food:	Snacks in Lanai City
Facilities:	Rest rooms and water at Lanai Airport and Lanai City

The ride to Shipwreck Beach on Lanai's northeast shore features a tour of Lanai City and a thrilling 7-mile descent on a narrow, winding road. The route takes advantage of the smoothest sections of Lanai's 32 miles of paved roads.

From the airport, ride north on Kamalapau Highway. This stretch of highway has rolling hills that take you from the center of the island up to Lanai City. The hills are fairly gentle, but the prevailing trade winds make the going difficult. Once in Lanai City and under protection of the mountains, the winds subside, and you can ease up on the pedals. Jim Dole created this town when he started his pineapple-growing operation on Lanai in the 1920s. At an elevation of nearly 1,700 feet, the town enjoys cooler temperatures than the rest of the island.

Throughout Lanai City are large Norfolk and Cooke Island pine trees. They were planted by naturalist George Munro in order to undo some of the damage inflicted upon the landscape by cattle ranching.

On the outskirts of Lanai City you will ride by the super-fancy Lodge at Koele, where an overnight stay will cost you sev-

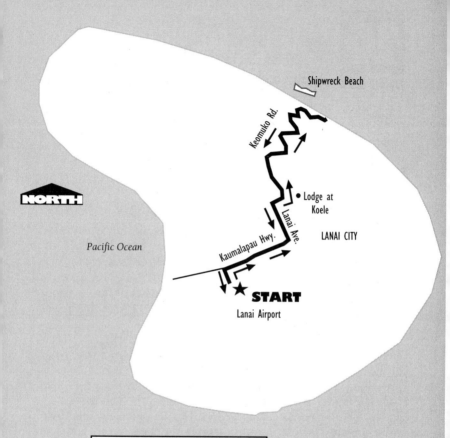

Shipwreck Beach

Keomuko Rd.

NORTH

Lodge at
Koele

Pacific Ocean

Lanai Ave.

Kaumalapau Hwy.

LANAI CITY

★ START

Lanai Airport

Getting There

Two airlines, Aloha and Hawaiian, fly to Lanai from Oahu and Maui. You can also access the island by ferry from Lahaina Harbor on the island of Maui.

DIREC-TIONS at a glance

0.0 Start from Lanai Airport and ride toward Kaumalapau Highway.

0.5 Turn right onto Kaumalapau Highway.

3.5 Turn left onto Lanai Avenue.

4.8 Lanai Highway bends to the left and becomes Keomuko Road.

12.2 Turnaround point at Shipwreck Beach

19.6 Keomuko Road bends to the right and becomes Lanai Avenue.

20.9 Turn right onto Kaumalapau Highway.

23.9 Turn left onto the Lanai Airport access road.

24.4 Return to Lanai Airport.

eral hundred dollars. The lodge is one of the two luxury resorts that have replaced pineapple as Lanai's major industry.

Leaving the lodge and the quiet town behind, Keomuko Road takes you over a ridge, then sends you plunging down to Shipwreck Beach. The road to the beach is narrow, but you won't find much traffic because only a few fishermen and an occasional tourist use it. The road is smooth, and you will find it's easy to pick up plenty of speed despite a strong headwind.

Spectacular views of Molokai and Maui are possible from the road, and the climate becomes drier as you roll away from Lanai's cool mountain region. The pines of Lanai City are replaced by trees permanently bent from the unrelenting trade winds. Between Molokai and Maui, the Pacific Ocean stretches out like rippling blue linoleum.

Keep a sharp eye out for the World War II shipwreck that is visible from the road at 9.8 miles from the beginning of your ride. The large brown ship rests parallel to the coastline. (You will not be able to see the ship from the bottom of the road unless you ride the jeep trail that runs about 2 miles up the coast.)

The pavement ends in a thicket of kiawe trees. If you have a mountain bike, you may choose to explore the dirt roads that follow the coastline in either direction. Be prepared, however, to deal with kiawe thorns. Well-adapted to dry climates, kiawe trees were introduced to Hawaii in 1828 to provide fuel, lumber, animal food, and flowers. Unfortunately, the tree also drops thorns that are exceptionally well-suited to puncturing bicycle tires.

Climbing back to Lanai City is not as bad as you might expect. The trade winds actually blow you up the hill. They also help as you make your way downhill from Lanai City to the airport.

Pineapple Memories
Manele Bay

Number of miles:	23.6
Approximate pedaling time:	3 hours
Terrain:	Hill
Traffic:	Light
Things to see:	Manele Bay Resort, Hulopoe Beach Park, Manele Bay Small Boat Harbor, former pineapple fields
Food:	Meals and snacks in Lanai City
Facilities:	Water and rest rooms at Hulopoe Beach Park

Lanai was known as the Pineapple Island until 1993, when the Dole Corporation decided to phase out its Lanai pineapple operation and shifted its efforts to the Philippines and Thailand, where labor costs are lower. Tourism is helping to replace the pineapple industry, and two luxury resorts now operate on the island: the Lodge at Koele and the Manele Bay Resort. Lanai Airport, which once seemed to resemble a bus stop, has been remodeled and now greets visitors with special touches like decorated cement floors and designer wall tiles.

As you leave the airport, you will notice fields of pineapple on either side of the road. These pineapples are mostly for decoration and for local consumption. There was a time when much of the island was covered with fields like these. Nowadays, grass and weeds have taken over.

Heading north on Kaumalapau Highway, you will have to ride against rolling hills and a brisk headwind. A right turn onto Manele Road takes you downhill and across Lanai's central plateau. This area's hardy soil is excellent for agriculture, but it

can sustain only a limited number of cattle. The weeds now grow thickly, and the only reminders of the pineapple industry are half-buried shreds of the black plastic ground cloth that once surrounded the plants.

After passing through the former pineapple fields, Manele Road bends sharply to the left, then plunges down to Manele Bay. This road experiences the most traffic on the island, and its surface has a rough texture. As you fly downhill, you will leave behind the cool, wet climate of central Lanai and enter the arid coastal area.

Before you reach the bottom of the road, check out the Manele Bay Resort. The front entrance features an elegant, sparkling-blue fountain. Billionaire Bill Gates came to this resort to celebrate his wedding, and the prices for an overnight stay reflect his buying power. From the beautifully landscaped lawns to the weathered sea-green barrel-tiled roof, this place does its best to make you feel good about spending several hundred dollars for an overnight stay.

Down the road a bit farther is Hulopoe Beach Park, which often sees visitors from Maui who come by boat and spend the day swimming, relaxing in the sun, or playing volleyball. The boats land at nearby Manele Bay Small Boat Harbor. The park and harbor area is in a conservation zone where fishing is controlled. You can spend a good part of the day exploring the beach before making your way back to the airport.

The ride to the airport is an abrupt climb that is very hot due to limited cloud cover and lack of shade from the low-growing shrubs. The road saps your strength, and the only relief comes from a few wandering breezes. About halfway up the road, you will wish you were back at Manele Bay Resort, swimming in the fountain, but eventually the heat gives way as you return to Lanai's central plateau.

Riding under the shadow of Lanai's highest mountain, Lanai-hale, you will find the going easy until you reach a small hill on the outskirts of Lanai City. With this ascent completed and after a left turn onto Kaumalapau Highway, the rest is all downhill with a tailwind. Soon you will be back at the airport.

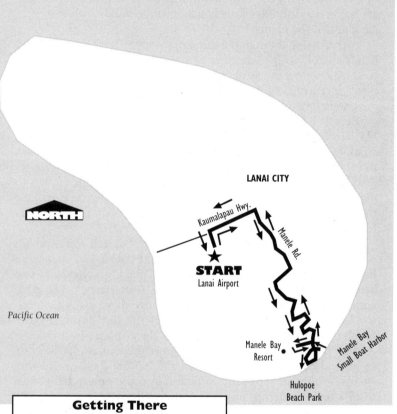

LANAI CITY

NORTH

Kaumalapau Hwy.

Manele Rd.

★ **START**
Lanai Airport

Pacific Ocean

Manele Bay
Resort

Manele Bay
Small Boat Harbor

Hulopoe
Beach Park

Getting There

Two airlines, Aloha and Hawaiian, fly to Lanai from Oahu and Maui. You can also access the island by ferry from Lahaina Harbor on the island of Maui.

**DIREC-
TIONS
at a glance**

0.0	Start your ride from the Lanai Airport and ride toward Kaumalapau Highway.
0.5	Turn right onto Kaumalapau Highway.
3.2	Turn right onto Manele Road.
6.9	Manele Road takes a sharp bend to the left.
10.0	Turn right into the Manele Bay Resort.
10.4	Turn around and retrace your route to Manele Road.
10.8	Turn right onto Manele Road.
11.2	Turn right to Hulopoe Beach Park.
11.6	Turn around and retrace your route to Manele Road.
12.0	Turn right into Manele Bay Small Boat Harbor.
12.25	Turn around and retrace your route to Manele Road.
12.5	Turn right onto Manele Road and begin your ascent back to Lanai's central plateau.
16.4	After the stop sign, turn right, staying on Manele Road.
20.1	Turn left onto Kaumalapau Highway.
23.1	Turn left onto the airport access road.
23.6	Return to Lanai Airport.

Riding to the Beach Landing
Kaunakakai

Number of miles:	17.2
Approximate pedaling time:	2.5 hours
Terrain:	Rolling hills
Traffic:	Light
Things to see:	Kaunakakai town, panoramic views of Molokai's undeveloped coast, views of Lanai
Food:	Meals and snacks at Kaunakakai and at the airport
Facilities:	Rest rooms and water at Kaunakakai and at the airport

Molokai has seen little development, and nowhere is this more evident than in Kaunakakai. This small town, the center of Molokai's population, is still without the franchised clothing stores and the sandwich shops that crowd the other major islands.

Getting to Kaunakakai from the Hoolehua Airport is a simple affair. Just ride east on Maunaloa Highway until you enter the center of town 7.6 miles later. The highway has shoulders and smooth pavement the whole way to Kaunakakai, and it's likely you will find the drivers on the road very courteous.

The highway starts off with gentle rolling hills that take you away from Molokai's western plateau; then it plunges down to sea level after crossing Kahuaawi Gulch. If the weather is clear, you can see the island of Lanai across Kalohi Channel as you descend into town.

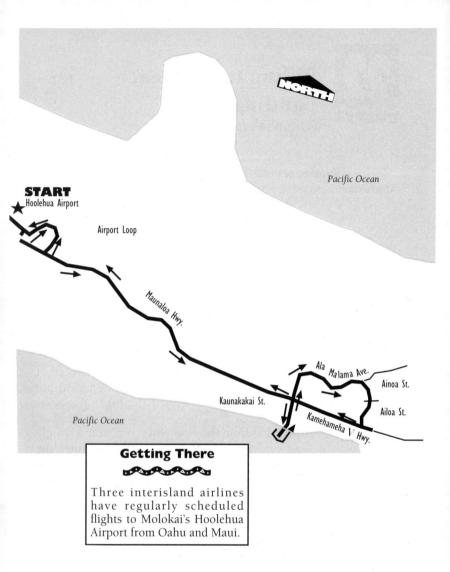

NORTH

Pacific Ocean

START
★ Hoolehua Airport

Airport Loop

Maunaloa Hwy.

Ala Malama Ave.

Ainoa St.

Ailoa St.

Kaunakakai St.

Kamehameha V Hwy.

Pacific Ocean

Getting There

Three interisland airlines have regularly scheduled flights to Molokai's Hoolehua Airport from Oahu and Maui.

DIREC-TIONS at a glance

0.0 From Hoolehua Airport, turn right onto Airport Loop.

0.8 Turn left onto Maunaloa Highway.

7.6 Turn right onto Kaunakakai Street, which takes you to the pier.

8.3 Turn around at the end of the pier, and retrace your route back into town.

9.0 After the stop sign, proceed straight at the intersection onto Ala Malama Avenue.

9.2 Turn right onto Ainoa Street, which becomes Ailoa Street.

9.4 Turn right onto Kamehameha V Highway, which becomes Maunaloa Highway.

16.4 Turn right onto Airport Loop.

17.2 Turn left into Hoolehua Airport.

In Kaunakakai, ride to the end of the wharf for views of Lanai and of Molokai's undeveloped coastline. One can imagine this is what Oahu must have looked like before the hotels were built in Waikiki.

Molokai is a narrow island, only 10 miles wide and 38 miles long. Kaunakakai is roughly in the middle of the island, on the southern coast. The area surrounding Kaunakakai is fairly dry as most of the rain falls on the east side of the island and on the windward side of Kamakou, Molokai's highest mountain. It takes only a few minutes to tour the town, which has very little in the way of entertainment or luxury accommodations.

Only one resort exists on the island, and it's far away on the western side of the island. Kaunakakai has neither skyscrapers nor stoplights, and most of the 7,000 residents of Molokai probably prefer it to remain that way.

In the peace and quiet of rural Molokai, residents busy themselves with fishing, hunting, ranching, and farming. Many people have side jobs to help make ends meet. A farmhand or a shopkeeper might double as a tour guide during the November-to-April tourist season.

Pineapple used to be the dominant economic force on the island, but the industry has since closed down, leaving grass and weeds to swallow up the fruit that was left rotting in the fields. Molokai farmers are busy looking for replacement crops like macadamia nuts and coffee, and there has even been some success with watermelon.

The ride back to the airport is a chore. In the afternoon heat, Maunaloa Highway will have you out of your saddle and sweating hard until you reach the rolling hills near the airport. The land along the highway is sparsely populated, and the vegetation is low-lying scrub and grass. Eventually, Hoolehua Airport welcomes you back with the sound of airplane engines and with breezes from the northeast.

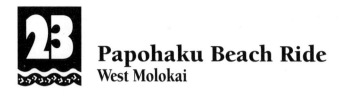

Papohaku Beach Ride
West Molokai

Number of miles:	26.1
Approximate pedaling time:	3 hours
Terrain:	Rolling hills
Traffic:	Light
Things to see:	Papohaku Beach Park, views of Oahu's east shore, West Molokai mountains
Food:	Meals and snacks at Hoolehua Airport
Facilities:	Rest rooms and water at the airport and at Papohaku Beach Park

The best country roads in the state can be found near Papohaku Beach on Molokai's west shore. This is where the sun shines brightly, and few cars compete with you for space on the roads.

From Hoolehua Airport, ride west on Maunaloa Highway. The highway has shoulders, and the riding is easy as you approach the foothills of the West Molokai mountains. West Molokai is the dry side of the island, and its worn-down mountains create a barrier to the shoreline. Along the highway are very few houses and little sign of development. Central and West Molokai once accommodated vast fields of pineapple, but those days are gone.

The climb over the mountains begins 3 miles from the airport and lasts until mile 6. Reward for your hard work comes in the form of a downhill run after turning from the highway onto Kaluakoi Road. The pavement on Kaluakoi is fractured like eggshells, and it creaks as you roll over it. It can be ridden safely, but the broken pavement prevents you from really picking up speed. This condition disappears once you pass the Kaluakoi Resort.

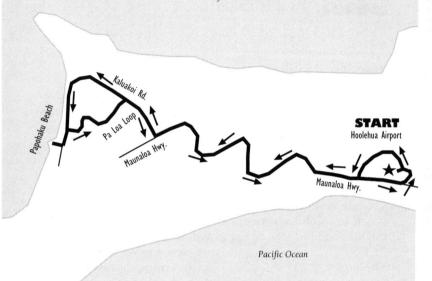

Pacific Ocean

Kaluakoi Rd.

Pa Loa Loop

Papohaku Beach

Maunaloa Hwy.

START
Hoolehua Airport

Maunaloa Hwy.

Pacific Ocean

Getting There

Three interisland airlines have regularly scheduled flights to Molokai's Hoolehua Airport from Oahu and Maui.

0.0 Turn left from Hoolehua Airport onto Airport Loop.

1.3 Turn right onto Maunaloa Highway

7.9 Turn right onto Kaluakoi Road.

13.4 Turn right into Papohaku Beach Park.

13.6 Turn around and leave the park by the way you came in.

13.8 Turn left onto Kaluakoi Road.

14.1 Turn right onto Pa Loa Loop.

15.4 Turn right onto Kaluakoi Road.

18.5 Turn left onto Maunaloa Highway.

25.3 Turn left onto Airport Loop.

26.1 Turn left into Hoolehua Airport.

Beyond the trees that line Kaluakoi Road, vegetation consists mostly of grass and introduced plants like haole koa and kiawe, which are well-suited to arid climates. At Papohaku Beach Park, you will find rest rooms and shady kiawe trees. The park is a perfect place for a quiet picnic before starting back. Be wary of the kiawe thorns, which love to stick into bicycle tires. Beyond the kiawe trees you will find a beautiful white sand beach, from which you can see Oahu across Kaiwi Channel.

As you sit with your feet in the sand on the quiet shores of Molokai, it's fun to imagine the crowds and the cars rushing about on the busy streets of Oahu. The rat race does not exist on Papohaku Beach, where the only footprints on the sand are probably your own.

After you leave the park, the sharp climb back to Maunaloa Highway will snap you back to reality. The route takes you past several large homes. Small signs advertising a local realty company and empty cul de sacs suggest the area is preparing for major development. Yet there's little evidence of activity, and the streets are quiet. Perhaps market conditions will change. People will buy the houses, and the roads will be put to more use. But for now, enjoy the streets while they are still quiet and empty.

When you turn from Kaluakoi Road back onto Maunaloa Highway, the most difficult climbing is behind you. The only thing that lies between you and the airport is the last of the low-lying West Molokai mountains. The grade going back is much easier than what you experienced coming out. Once you reach the top of the hill, smooth roads allow a high-speed descent to Molokai's central plateau. Brisk northeasterly winds usually blow across this section of the island, so expect to be battling a headwind on your way back to Hoolehua Airport.

Kalaupapa Overlook
Hoolehua to Palaau Park

Number of miles:	18.1
Approximate pedaling time:	2.5 hours
Terrain:	Hills
Traffic:	Light
Things to see:	Meyer Sugar Mill, Kalaupapa Lookout, Phallic Rock, Palaau State Park
Food:	Meals and snacks at the airport and Kualapuu town
Facilities:	Rest rooms and water at the airport, rest rooms at Kalaupapa Lookout

Now that modern medicine has found a way to treat Hansen's disease (leprosy), it's easy to look at the Kalaupapa Peninsula and enjoy its great beauty. In the past, however, just the name of this isolated place, where many people infected with the disease were banished, conjured feelings of dread.

Riding to Palaau State Park, where you can look down to the peninsula, requires a climb into Molokai's mountainous interior. From the airport you will ride rolling hills on Maunaloa Highway until you turn left on Kalae Highway and begin the steady climb to the park. The narrow highway does not have much in the way of shoulders. As you reach higher elevations, dry shrubs and grass give way to green trees and pastures.

Molokai is a study in climatic extremes. On the eastern tip are tropical rain forests; the western tip is hot and dry. Palaau State Park is in the transition zone between these two climates. In this area it's common to be riding on a sunny day, then suddenly find yourself drenched by a passing shower. When water

meets hot asphalt, it creates steam that wisps above the road and carries the scent of fresh rain into the air.

There is cattle ranching in this area. It's common to see horses tied up along the roadside, performing their lawn mowing duties while cows do the same in protected pastures behind them.

After passing by the Ironwood Hills Golf Course, you may want to stop and investigate the Meyer Sugar Mill, located on the left at 8.3 miles into this ride. The restored mill dates back to 1878, and it's a good diversion from your climb to Palaau State Park.

The Kukuiohapuu Mule Trail begins on your right just before you reach the park. The trail, about 3 miles long, drops nearly 1,600 feet down to Kalaupapa Peninsula. Permission is required to go on the trail and to tour Kalaupapa. Arrangements can be made through Damien Tours (808–576–6171).

A small gravel trail leads from the parking lot at Palaau State Park to the Kalaupapa Lookout. The lookout provides a fine view of the peninsula, plus displays on the history of the Kalaupapa leprosy colony. The first sign of the disease in Hawaii appeared in 1840, and it spread quickly though the native population. In 1868, Kalaupapa was designated as a leprosy settlement, and people with the disease were rounded up and forcibly sent there.

While you are in Hawaii you will probably hear the praises of Father Damien more than once. Originally from Belgium, Damien came voluntarily to Kalaupapa, risking infection, to care for those with leprosy. He devoted his life to those condemned to Kalaupapa, bringing order to the community and easing the people's suffering by caring for them and building shelters. Damien died in 1889 of leprosy.

Palaau State Park also features the famous Phallic Rock, found at the end of a small trail just off the parking lot. A plaque near the rock tells an intriguing story.

The ride is easygoing once you leave the park. After a quick downhill run on Kalae Highway, the route flattens out on Far-

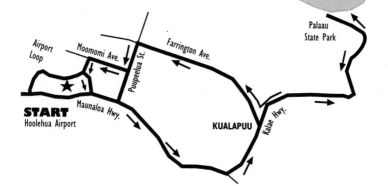

NORTH

Pacific Ocean

Kalaupapa Peninsula

Kalaupapa Lookout

Palaau
State Park

Airport
Loop

Moomomi Ave.

Farrington Ave.

Puupeelua St.

START
Hoolehua Airport

Maunaloa Hwy.

KUALAPUU

Kalae Hwy.

Getting There

Three interisland airlines
have regularly scheduled
flights to Molokai's Hoolehua
Airport from Oahu and Maui.

DIREC-TIONS at a glance

0.0	From Hoolehua Airport turn right onto Airport Loop.
0.8	Turn left onto Maunaloa Highway.
3.5	Turn left onto Kalae Highway
9.4	Turn around at Palaau State Park, and retrace your route on Kalae Highway.

13.4 Turn right onto Farrington Avenue.
15.8 Turn left onto Puupeelua Street.
16.5 Turn right onto Moomomi Avenue.
17.4 Turn left onto Mokulele Street.
17.6 Turn right onto Airport Loop.
18.1 Turn left into Hoolehua Airport.

rington Avenue, where you can see coffee bushes growing near Kualapuu Reservoir. A coffee shop on your right is a good place to stop for a break. The last few miles to the airport are classic rural Molokai, with quaint one-story homes, some free-range chickens, and a loose dog or two.

Trek to the East
Kaluaaha and Halawa

Number of miles:	28.4 (54.2 for Halawa Valley ride)
Approximate pedaling time:	3 hours (6 hours for Halawa Valley ride)
Terrain:	Flat (hills for Halawa Valley ride)
Traffic:	Light
Things to see:	Kukui nut trees, Our Lady of Sorrows Church, deserted beaches, ancient fishponds, views of West Maui, Halawa Valley
Food:	Meals and snacks in Kaunakakai
Facilities:	Rest rooms and water at Kaunakakai Regional Community Park

Riding east on Kamehameha V Highway is fun because the road is flat and smooth, and it's easy to ride fast. Hawaiian fishponds are the hidden feature on this ride for the first 14 miles. Look for them carefully on your right, where they appear in the ocean just off shore.

Lack of development on Molokai has left many archaeological sites largely undisturbed, and of all the sites, Molokai's fishponds are the most interesting. To the casual observer the ponds seem unremarkable, but to the Hawaiians they were very special. Some of the ponds, like Keawa Nui, have been in use since the 1500s.

Fish has always been an integral part of the Hawaiian diet, and in 1901 there were more than one hundred fishponds operating in the islands. The Hawaiians built more than sixty ponds on Molokai's southeast shore. Ancient fishponds are now under attack by aggressive foreign plants such as mangrove and by pressure from developers who want to use coastal areas in different ways. The people of Molokai have worked hard to retain their fishponds, and a renewed interest in aquaculture by residents and by scientists from the University of Hawaii has kept some of them in operation.

On the mountain side of the highway you will see kiawe trees, with an occasional kukui nut tree hidden between them. Exercise caution around kiawe trees, because they drop thorns that puncture bicycle tires. Kukui nut trees, on the other hand, pose no such danger. For the ancient Hawaiians, the kukui had many uses. The trunks were used to make canoes. The bark was made into dye to decorate clothing. The nut kernels were burned as candles, or prepared as a relish and eaten. The nut shells can be polished and strung into beautiful leis. The kukui has been designated as the state tree.

The turnaround point for the ride to Kaluaaha comes at Our Lady of Sorrows Church, on the left at 14.2 miles east of Kaunakakai. The original church that stood here was built in 1874 by Father Damien, the priest who lived with the people who were banished to the Kalaupapa leprosy settlement. You can turn around here for the return ride to Kaunakakai. But if you would rather spend the rest of the day exploring the coast, continue east on Kamehameha V Highway to Halawa Valley.

In the miles beyond Our Lady of Sorrows, the highway becomes more and more narrow as it snakes along the coast. Eventually it dwindles to a single lane with many blind turns and steep hills. To your right, only 8 miles across Pailolo Channel, Maui is plainly visible.

As you near Halawa Valley, the road turns away from the coast and begins a steady uphill climb, not relenting until you pass a small landing strip. Once at the top of the ridge, the rest of the way to Halawa is downhill.

Halawa Valley is a pristine tropical paradise that benefits from an abundance of rainfall. Archaeological evidence suggests that the valley was inhabited by Hawaiians as far back as A.D. 600. The valley is undeveloped, aside from a few houses near

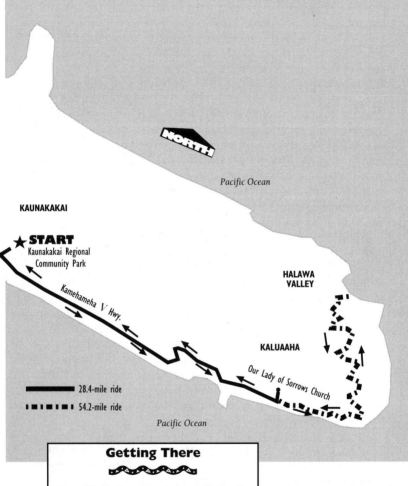

KAUNAKAKAI

Pacific Ocean

★ START
Kaunakakai Regional
Community Park

HALAWA
VALLEY

Kamehameha V Hwy.

KALUAAHA

Our Lady of Sorrows Church

——————— 28.4-mile ride
▪ ▬ ▪ ▬ ▪ ▬ ▪ 54.2-mile ride

Pacific Ocean

Getting There

From Hoolehua Airport, travel 7 miles
east on Maunaloa Highway to Kaunakakai Regional Community Park.
The park appears on your left and is
plainly visible from the road.

DIREC-TIONS
at a glance

28.4-mile ride
- 0.0 From Kaunakakai Regional Community Park, turn left onto Kamehameha V Highway and ride east.
- 14.2 At Our Lady of Sorrows Church, located on the left, turn around and retrace your route on Kamehameha Highway.
- 28.4 Turn right into Kaunakakai Regional Community Park.

54.2-mile ride
- 0.0 From Kaunakakai Regional Community Park, turn left onto Kamehameha V Highway and ride east.
- 27.1 Turn around at Halawa Valley and retrace your route back to Kaunakakai.
- 54.2 Turn right into Kaunakakai Regional Community Park.

the bay, and it's surprising that a place that is so accessible remains unspoiled.

The ride back to Kaunakakai goes quickly. The trade winds blow favorably in this direction, and once the hills are out of the way, you can really fly down the road.

Into the Mountains
Waihee to Iao Valley

Number of miles:	16.4
Approximate pedaling time:	2.5 hours
Terrain:	Rolling hills
Traffic:	Heavy traffic on Main Street and Kaahumanu Avenue
Things to see:	Waihee Beach Park, Kepaniwai Heritage Gardens, Iao Needle
Food:	Meals and snacks in Kahului
Facilities:	Rest rooms and water at Wailuku War Memorial Park, Waihee Beach Park, Kepaniwai Heritage Gardens, and Iao Valley State Park

Brooding in a layer of dark gray clouds for most of the year, the mountains of West Maui form an impressive backdrop to the communities nearby. These mountains are only half as tall as Mount Haleakala on the eastern side of the island, but they are incredibly beautiful with their steep green cliffs and narrow V-shaped valleys.

Before heading into the mountains, explore Waihee Beach Park, situated off Kahekili Highway. On the way to Waihee from Wailuku War Memorial Park, the terrain is mostly flat and un-challenging. Finding the beach park can be a task, because it's hidden at the end of two unmarked roads. The first road appears on the maps as Halewaiu Road, and it's your first right after passing the Waihee baseball park.

Halewaiu Road goes downhill past a small neighborhood and ends at the Waiehu Municipal Golf Course parking lot. Ride to the beach park via a small road that starts at the left side of the

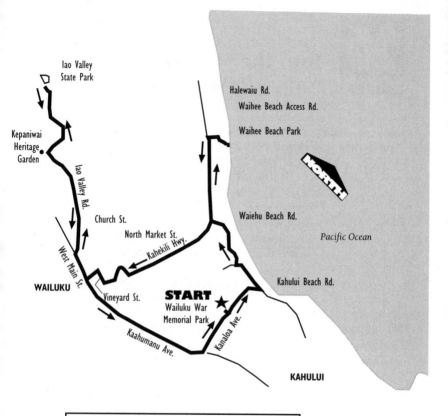

Iao Valley
State Park

Kepaniwai
Heritage
Garden

Iao Valley Rd.

West Main St.

Church St.

North Market St.

Kahekili Hwy.

WAILUKU

Vineyard St.

Kaahumanu Ave.

Kanaloa Ave.

START
Wailuku War
Memorial Park

Halewaiu Rd.

Waihee Beach Access Rd.

Waihee Beach Park

NORTH

Waiehu Beach Rd.

Pacific Ocean

Kahului Beach Rd.

KAHULUI

Getting There

Coming from Kahului Airport, turn right onto Haleakala Highway, then right again onto Hana Highway, which becomes Kaahumanu Avenue. Wailuku War Memorial Park will be on your right, after you pass Maui Community College.

0.0 From Wailuku War Memorial Park turn left onto Kanaloa Avenue, and ride north.

0.7 Turn left onto Kahului Beach Road.

0.9 Turn right onto Waiehu Beach Road.

2.5 Turn right onto Kahekili Highway.

3.7 Turn right onto Halewaiu Road, which leads to Waiehu Municipal Golf Course parking lot.

4.3 From the golf course parking lot, turn left onto the Waihee Beach access road.

4.6 Turn around at Waihee Beach Park, and leave by the way you came in.

4.9 Turn right, back into Waiehu Municipal Golf Course parking lot.

5.0 Turn left onto Halewaiu Road.

5.5 Turn left onto Kahekili Highway, which later becomes North Market Street.

8.8 Turn right onto Vineyard Street.

8.9 Turn left onto Church Street.

9.0 Turn right onto West Main Street.

9.7 Veer right onto Iao Valley Road.

12.0 Turn around at Iao Valley State Park, and retrace your route on Iao Valley Road.

14.4 After stopping at the sign, merge left, back onto West Main Street, which becomes Kaahumanu Avenue.

16.1 Turn left onto Kanaloa Avenue.

16.4 Turn left, and return to Wailuku War Memorial Park.

parking lot. This road is often slippery with patches of loose sand and is marked only by a tiny sign that says SHORE ACCESS. At the park you will find picnic tables, rest rooms, and a white sand beach. It's a beautiful place to watch the surf come in and to feel the strong northeasterly trade winds.

Return to Kahekili Highway, and ride south toward Iao Valley. This stretch of highway is smooth and pleasant. After a short downhill dip, you climb into the town of Wailuku, and the highway becomes North Market Street.

Wailuku has a blend of structures that includes modern office buildings and some old wooden storefronts. The town has a supermarket, a McDonald's, government offices, and a variety of small businesses. West Main Street cuts through the heart of downtown Wailuku and goes uphill to Iao Valley Road.

Riding into Iao Valley is like entering a green mountain cathedral. Iao Valley Road initially goes downhill from its junction with West Main Street. Then it's a steady climb until you reach the back of the valley, where you will find two public parks. Along the way you will see a few homes and many kukui nut trees.

The first of the two parks is Kepaniwai Heritage Gardens, which appears on your left at 11.5 miles into the day's ride. On the park grounds are structures built to reflect the cultures of the varied peoples who came to Hawaii. New England, Hawaiian, Spanish, Chinese, and Japanese architectural styles are among those represented. Picnic areas are provided between the ethnic displays.

Iao Valley Road is steepest between the heritage gardens and Iao Valley State Park. As you make this final climb, watch for the rock formation on the right that looks like John Kennedy's profile. It's marked with a sign on the road, and tour buses stop to give visitors a chance to see this bizarre attraction. Whether or not you can make out the Kennedy profile, it's a good excuse to stop and catch your breath.

The park provides an open view of the mountains that rise up from the valley, and it features Iao Needle, a sharp and prominent spire. Below Iao Needle, streams pour across mossy rocks on their journey along the valley floor. The great natural beauty of the area makes it easy to understand why ancient Hawaiians considered Iao Valley sacred and why they used the area as a burying place for their chiefs.

High Times on Maui
Haleakala and Makawao

Number of miles:	29 miles (83.5 for Haleakala summit ride)
Approximate pedaling time:	3.5 hours (7 hours for Haleakala summit ride)
Terrain:	Mountains
Traffic:	Heavy traffic on Hana Highway
Things to see:	Working sugar mill, Paia town, Makawao town, Haleakala Crater
Food:	Meals and snacks in Kahului, Makawao, and Paia
Facilities:	Water and rest rooms at Kahului Park and in Makawao

When the morning sun rises over Haleakala, the sky is lit with soothing shafts of light that pierce the clouds and pool on the earth below. Gradually the sugarcane and pineapple fields, pastures, small towns, and winding roads are awakened by the warmth of the sun, and a new day begins on Maui.

Haleakala makes a sunrise special. This mountain, third highest in the state, encompasses the entire east side of Maui. Its name in Hawaiian means "house of the sun."

There are several ways to experience Haleakala. If you want to forgo the arduous trip to the summit, just ride as far as Makawao, a small town on the lower slopes of Haleakala. This option gives you a taste of what it's like to ride to the top, but it will return you to Kahului without sapping every ounce of your energy.

Then again, if you love climbing with your bike, just go for it. Start at sea level, following the directions to Makawao. From

PUU ULAULA
10,023 ft.
Above Sea Level

Haleakala
Crater Rd.

Park Headquarters

NORTH

Haleakala Hwy.

Kula Hwy.

Kealaloa Ave.

Hanamu Rd.

Olinda Rd.

KAHULUI

START
Kahului Park

MAKAWAO

Makawao Rd.

Haleakala Hwy.

Wakea Ave.

Onehee St.

For 29-mile ride turn right onto Makawao Ave.
To ride to the summit of Haleakala,
continue straight onto Olinda Rd.

Baldwin Ave.

Hana Hwy.

Kaahumanu Ave.

PAIA

Hana Hwy.

East Kamehameha Ave.

Pacific Ocean

Getting There

Coming from Kahului Airport, turn right
onto Haleakala Highway, then right again
onto Hana Highway. Turn left onto East
Kamehameha Avenue then right on West
Wakea Avenue. From West Wakea Avenue turn left onto Onehee Street. Ka-
halui Park will be on the left.

DIREC-TIONS at a glance

29-mile ride (round-trip to Makawao)

0.0   From Kahului Park, turn right onto One-hee Street.

0.4   Turn right onto West Wakea Avenue.

1.6   Turn right onto Hana Highway.

7.9   Turn right onto Baldwin Avenue.

14.9   Turn right onto Makawao Avenue.

16.6   Turn right onto Haleakala Highway.

23.8   Turn left onto Hana Highway.

27.5   Turn left onto East Kamehameha Avenue.

28.3   Turn right onto West Wakea Avenue.

28.6   Turn left onto Onehee Street.

29.0   Turn left into Kahului Park.

83.5-mile ride (round-trip to Haleakala summit)

0.0   Follow the directions for the 29-mile ride until you reach the end of Baldwin Avenue at 14.9 miles.

14.9   After the stop sign, proceed straight through the intersection onto Olinda Road.

15.1   Turn right onto Hanamu Road.

15.9   Turn left onto Kealaloa Avenue.

16.1   Turn left onto Haleakala Highway.

21.0   Turn left onto Haleakala Crater Road.

33.0   Stop at the ranger station, and pay your admission into Haleakala National Park.

43.0   Turn around at the top and retrace your route on Haleakala Crater Road.

65.0   Turn right onto Haleakala Highway.

70.9   Kula Highway merges with Haleakala Highway. Turn right, staying on Haleakala Highway.

78.3   Turn left onto Hana Highway.

82.0   Turn left onto East Kamehameha Avenue.

82.8 Turn right onto West Wakea Avenue.
83.1 Turn left onto Onehee Street.
83.5 Turn left into Kahului Park.

Makawao, continue the additional 28 miles to the summit, at an elevation of 10,023 feet.

Begin at Kahului Park, in the middle of Kahului's urban neighborhood. The first challenge is crossing the cane fields of Maui's central plain to the town of Paia. Here the northeasterly winds are very strong as they funnel between Haleakala and the mountains of West Maui. In Paia, however, the winds die down.

Baldwin Avenue marks the beginning of your ascent to Makawao. Early in this climb you will pass one of the few operating sugar mills remaining in the state. Baldwin Avenue is free of heavy traffic, but it lacks shoulders as it twists and turns uphill to Makawao.

Makawao is a tiny town with a business district of old wooden storefronts. You will find restaurants plus a variety of stores selling such items as wood stoves, groceries, rodeo equipment, and natural foods. The air is cooler at this elevation, and the town has a *paniolo*, or cowboy, feel to it.

At Makawao you can decide whether you want to continue climbing toward the Haleakala summit. If you decide to start back at this point, turn right from Baldwin Avenue onto Makawao Avenue, and begin your return trip to Kahului. Otherwise, continue straight onto Olinda Road, after making sure you have plenty of food and water for the climb and a jacket for the cool descent.

From Makawao, the rode to the summit can be divided into three stages. The first stage is from Olinda Road to the beginning of Haleakala Crater Road. This section is characterized by a brutal wall of asphalt on Olinda Road. This is the steepest part of the climb, and happily it ends as soon as you turn onto Hanamu Road.

The next section is from the beginning of Haleakala Crater Road to the ranger station at Haleakala National Park. This section of the ride is fairly steep, taking you above the residential areas and into open green pastures. The road has many switchbacks.

The final stage is the 10-mile climb from the ranger station to the summit. After you pay your entry fee, you leave the pastures behind and enter the park. This last stage is where you are most likely to experience chilling winds and clouds that reduce visibility. You will also start to feel the effects of the thinning air. Every muscle fiber in your body begins to slow down as you gasp for oxygen.

Views from the top are spectacular. Volcanic cinders with hues of red and brown bring out the contours of the crater below, and delicate water vapors seem to turn into clouds right before your eyes.

The only thing that compares with the view from the top is the ride down. Aside from a few bumpy cattle guards, the road is smooth sailing all the way to the bottom. Broad shoulders appear on Haleakala Highway after you pass Makawao Avenue, and when you finally have to start pedaling again on the outskirts of Kahului, there is a touch of sadness that the downhill was over with so quickly. Thankfully there is a remedy for this: another ride to the top.

Whale Watch
Lahaina

Number of miles:	28.8
Approximate pedaling time:	3.5 hours
Terrain:	Gentle hills near Maalaea Bay, otherwise flat
Traffic:	Heavy on Honoapiilani Highway
Things to see:	Lahaina town, West Maui Mountains, whales, views of the islands of Lanai, Kohoolawe, and Molokini
Food:	Snacks at Maalaea Store, meals and snacks in Lahaina
Facilities:	Water and rest rooms at Maalaea Bay and Lahaina

Humpback whales travel more than 3,500 miles to spend their winters in the warm waters of Hawaii. The Hawaiian Islands provide a protective area where whales can breed, calve, and nurse their young. This ride, which begins at Maalaea Bay and goes along Maui's western coast to Lahaina, has several points where you can stop and scan the ocean for whales. You will usually be able to see them between November and May.

From Maalaea Boat Harbor you begin by riding Honoapiilani Highway over a series of gentle hills. The highway goes along sea cliffs but eventually drops down to sea level. Along the way you will pass through a short, unlit tunnel, so make sure your bike has its required reflectors. Lights and reflective clothing will increase your margin of safety. Sections of this highway have been carved into the mountain, and curtains of chain-link fencing have been draped on the slopes to protect the highway from

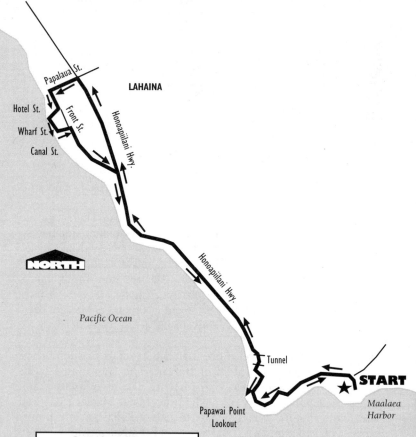

Papalaua St.

Hotel St.

Wharf St.

Canal St.

Front St.

LAHAINA

Honoapiilani Hwy.

NORTH

Pacific Ocean

Honoapiilani Hwy.

Tunnel

START

Maalaea Harbor

Papawai Point
Lookout

Getting There

From Wailuku travel 7 miles south on Honoapiilani Highway. Maalaea Boat Harbor will be on the left.

DIREC-TIONS at a glance

	0.0	From Maalaea Boat Harbor turn left onto Honoapiilani Highway and ride west.
	14.2	Turn left onto Papalaua Street.
	14.4	Turn left onto Front Street.
	14.8	Turn right onto Hotel Street.
	14.85	Turn left onto Wharf Street.
14.93		Turn left onto Canal Street.
14.98		Turn right onto Front Street.
15.9		Turn right onto Honoapiilani Highway.
28.8		Turn right into the Maalaea Boat Harbor.

falling rocks. This area, on the leeward side of the island, is fairly dry and arid.

The highway is busy with traffic, but there are smooth shoulders all the way to Lahaina. After passing the rolling hills, you will find yourself on flat land near the coast. Normal trade winds blow favorably in this direction, and before long you will be in Lahaina.

Lahaina was the capital of the Hawaiian Islands between 1820 and 1845. At the height of the whaling industry, Lahaina became a port of call for many whaling ships. When the industry died and the whalers left, Lahaina declined in importance, and soon the town was eclipsed by Honolulu.

Aside from a large hotel and fast-food establishments, Lahaina has tried to maintain its old style and feel. When you turn onto Front Street, you can imagine how it must have been when the area was jam-packed with sailors and merchants. The storefronts are wooden, and in some places there are wooden sidewalks. Most of the buildings are two stories high, and occasionally you can glimpse through the cross streets and see sugarcane fields behind Lahaina on the lower slopes of the West Maui Mountains.

Yet there is no denying this is a tourist town. At the harbor, whaling ships have been replaced by expensive yachts, and sailors have been replaced with eager tourists. Stores sell an endless variety of souvenirs, and near the harbor you will find artists selling their creations under a massive banyan tree with limbs that extend so far beyond its trunk that they must be supported by posts. Once past the visitor establishments on Front Street, you can see bungalows and quaint beach cottages, fading reminders of what Lahaina was like before mass tourism.

The ride back to Maalaea Bay starts off flat and easy as you pass by four small beach parks and along shores lined with pebbles. In this direction the trade winds blow against you, making the return journey seem longer. After you pass through the unlit tunnel, you will begin to climb the gentle hills that stand between you and Maalaea Boat Harbor. Along the way, stop at the viewpoints where you can look out and see the islands of Molokini, Kohoolawe, and Lanai.

These sea cliffs are also a prime location for viewing humpback whales. Despite the large size of the whales, it takes a good pair of binoculars to see them in the vast channel below. Patient viewers may see broad flukes rise out of the water as a whale dives, or even see a whale propel itself partway out of the water, creating an explosion of foam as it crashes back into the sea.

Luxury Ride
Kihei to Makena

Number of miles:	20.2
Approximate pedaling time:	2.5 hours
Terrain:	Rolling hills
Traffic:	Moderate traffic on Piilani Highway
Things to see:	Views of Mount Haleakala and the islands of Kahoolawe and Molokini
Food:	Meals and snacks at Kihei
Facilities:	Water and rest rooms at Mai Poina Oe Iau Park and Makena Beach Park

Situated next to the sea in the shadow of Haleakala, the town of Kihei enjoys warm weather and breezy trade winds. This area has seen much development over the years as resorts and housing developments were built, and more construction is on the way.

The ride begins at Mai Poina Oe Iau Park, which is dedicated to those who served in World War II. The name means "forget me not." The park has only a single bathroom and a few parking spaces, but the beach is beautiful.

From the shore you ride inland and turn onto Piilani Highway, where you will find generous shoulders and smooth pavement. At times, the shoulders are more than 12 feet wide, a rare luxury in Hawaii. This comfortable condition lasts for 6 miles.

As you ride, look at Haleakala on your left. This volcano is so massive that it takes no distinct shape as it rises out of sight above the clouds. The highway crosses gentle, rolling hills and is easy to ride. At 6.7 miles, the highway ends, and you turn right onto Wailea Ike Drive, which takes you downhill into the heart of the high-end resorts along the coast.

Along Wailea Alanui Road, look for the blue beach-access

signs if you want to explore the area's beaches. In Hawaii, beaches are public property, and hotels must provide access to the shore. This means you can enjoy the beach in front of a hotel just as easily as the person who spent big bucks to stay there.

The terrain is hilly as you ride farther down the coast, and the road is lined with the manicured trees and perfectly kept lawns of the resort area. On the left side of the road you will see people swinging clubs at Wailea Golf Course, and on the right you will see the grand entrances to expensive resorts.

Turning onto Makena Road takes you away from the resorts and leads to Makena Landing. The waters in this area are abundant with fish, and it's a popular place for scuba divers.

Off the coast of Maui you can see the crescent-shaped island called Molokini. One Hawaiian legend says the island was once the head of a lizard-like monster known as a moo (pronounced MO-oh). The moo infuriated Pele, the goddess of fire, when it disguised itself and became the wife of Lohiau, Pele's dream lover. In anger, Pele ripped the moo in two. Its head became Molokini, and its tail became Puu Olai, a nearby hill on Maui.

Molokini is part of a conservation district where fishing is not allowed. Tourists are brought in by boat to explore Molokini's reef and to swim among its fish.

Kahoolawe, the island that stands behind Molokini, is off limits to the public, protected by a 2-mile water perimeter enforced by the Coast Guard. From World War II until the late 1980s, the island served as a military practice target and was bombed with every conventional weapon in the U.S. Navy's arsenal. The island is now littered with unexploded ordnance.

The bombing stopped after many years of protest by a group called the Save Kahoolawe Ohana, and the Navy has since returned control of the island to the State of Hawaii. Plans to restore parts of Kahoolawe are under way, with the Navy paying for the work.

The hill on Wailea Ike Drive is the only major obstacle on the return ride to your starting point at the beach park, and familiar roads make the trip easy.

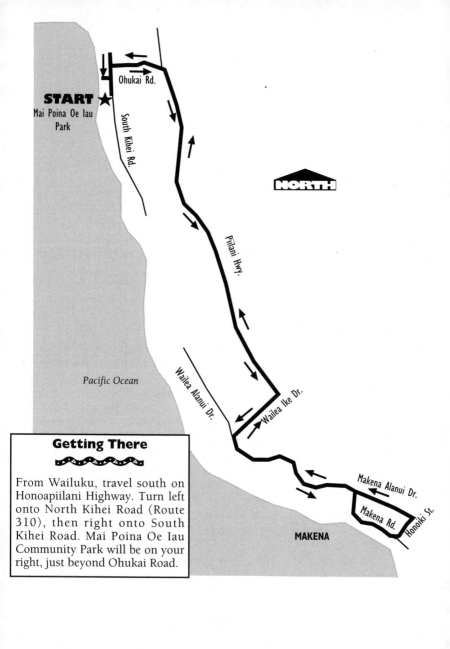

START ★
Mai Poina Oe Iau
Park

Ohukai Rd.

South Kihei Rd.

NORTH

Piilani Hwy.

Pacific Ocean

Wailea Alanui Dr.

Wailea Ike Dr.

Makena Alanui Dr.

Makena Rd.

Honoiki St.

MAKENA

Getting There

From Wailuku, travel south on Honoapiilani Highway. Turn left onto North Kihei Road (Route 310), then right onto South Kihei Road. Mai Poina Oe Iau Community Park will be on your right, just beyond Ohukai Road.

DIREC-TIONS
at a glance

0.0 From Mai Poina Oe Iau Park, turn left onto South Kihei Road and ride north.

0.03 Turn right onto Ohukai Road.

0.5 Turn right onto Piilani Highway.

6.7 Turn right onto Wailea Ike Drive.

7.4 Turn left onto Wailea Alanui Drive, which becomes Makena Alanui Drive.

9.4 Turn right onto Makena Road.

10.0 Turn left onto Honoiki Street.

10.2 Turn left onto Makena Alanui Road.

12.8 Turn right onto Wailea Ike Drive.

13.5 Turn left onto Piilani Highway.

19.7 Turn left onto Ohukai Road.

20.2 Turn left onto South Kihei Road.

20.23 Return to Mai Poina Oe Iau Park.

Bicycling the Big Island
Hilo to Akaka Falls

Number of miles:	34.0
Approximate pedaling time:	4 hours
Terrain:	Rolling hills with one steep climb
Traffic:	Moderately heavy on Hawaii Belt Road
Things to see:	Hilo Bay, Pepeekeo Scenic Drive, Hawaii Tropical Botanical Garden, Akaka Falls
Food:	Snacks in Hilo, Honomu, and on Pepeekeo Scenic Drive
Facilities:	Rest rooms and water at Hoolulu Park and Akaka Falls Park

People say it always rains in Hilo on the Big Island of Hawaii, and for most of the year they're right. Hilo, the biggest town on Hawaii, is on the side of the island that greets the moisture-laden trade winds first. Rain makes Hilo beautiful and green. After an early-morning rain shower, sunlight peeks through the clouds and reflects off every shiny leaf. As the countryside is dripping dry, you can almost feel the plants drawing the water in and growing.

This ride begins at Hoolulu Park in Hilo and continues north along the coast to Akaka Falls Park. At the beginning you will find yourself close the ocean on Bayfront Highway, passing a beach with dark-colored sand flecked with tiny bits of glitter. Past the beach area is a slippery, metal-surfaced bridge. Wet weather makes this bridge dangerous for bicycles, so heed the signs that direct cyclists to walk their bikes across.

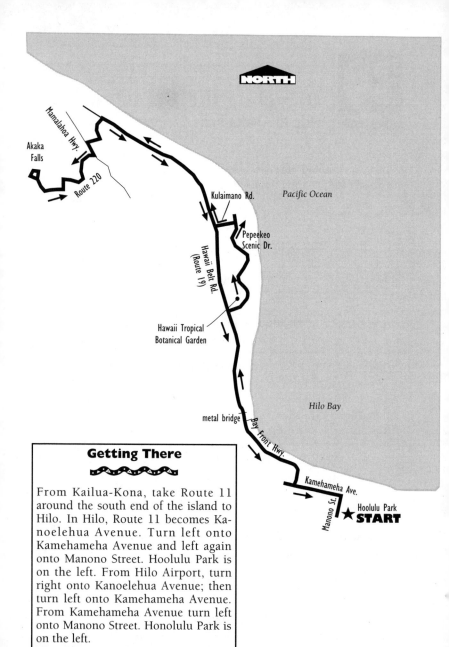

NORTH

Mamalahoa Hwy.

Akaka
Falls

Route 220

Kulaimano Rd.

Pepeekeo
Scenic Dr.

Pacific Ocean

Hawaii Belt Rd.
(Route 19)

Hawaii Tropical
Botanical Garden

Hilo Bay

metal bridge

Bay Front Hwy.

Kamehameha Ave.

Manono St.

Hoolulu Park
★ START

Getting There

From Kailua-Kona, take Route 11
around the south end of the island to
Hilo. In Hilo, Route 11 becomes Kanoelehua Avenue. Turn left onto
Kamehameha Avenue and left again
onto Manono Street. Hoolulu Park is
on the left. From Hilo Airport, turn
right onto Kanoelehua Avenue; then
turn left onto Kamehameha Avenue.
From Kamehameha Avenue turn left
onto Manono Street. Honolulu Park is
on the left.

DIREC-TIONS at a glance

0.0 From Hoolulu Park turn right onto Manono Street.

0.2 Turn left onto Kamehameha Avenue.

0.7 Turn onto Bayfront Highway, which becomes Hawaii Belt Road (Route 19).

6.2 Turn right onto Pepeekeo Scenic Drive.

9.8 Turn left onto Kulaimano Road.

10.2 Turn right onto Hawaii Belt Road.

13.7 Turn left onto Route 220.

14.1 Turn left onto Mamalahoa Highway.

14.3 Turn right onto Route 220.

17.6 Turn around at Akaka Falls Park, and retrace your route back to Mamalahoa Highway.

21.0 Turn left onto Mamalahoa Highway.

21.2 Turn right onto Route 220.

21.6 Turn right onto Hawaii Belt Road.

33.3 Turn left onto Kamehameha Avenue.

33.8 Turn right onto Manono Street.

34.0 Turn left into Hoolulu Park.

Once over the bridge, you put Hilo behind you, and the road begins to climb uphill. Look for the scenic viewpoint on your right, which gives an excellent view of Hilo Bay.

Farther along Hawaii Belt Road you will find the countryside thinly populated, with modest homes near the road. On clear days you can catch a glimpse of the scientific observatories on top of Mauna Kea, which looms far in the distance on your left. The road continues its gentle climb until Pepeekeo Scenic Drive.

On Pepeekeo, you will say goodbye to the sounds of trucks and roaring traffic, and in its place you will hear birds chirping and water gurgling over mossy rocks in shady mountain streams. This piece of road is a remnant of the old highway that used to go around the island, and you will find it packed with wonderful sights. On the left, look for a small white cottage where you can sign up for guided tours of the nearby Hawaii Tropical Botanical Garden.

This 4-mile scenic road takes you up and down a few manageable hills. Along the road you will see pandanas, kukui nut, guava, and palm trees. Rocky sea cliffs and the deep blue waters of Onomea Bay complement the lush green scenery. There are several small stores along the way where you can pick up a refreshing drink.

Relax while you can on the scenic drive because after you rejoin Hawaii Belt Road and turn onto Route 220, you will begin a steep climb up to Akaka Falls Park. The road climbs to an elevation of 1,600 feet in less than 4 miles. The first stage of the climb, from the beginning of Route 220 to Mamalahoa Highway, is very steep. Once on Mamalahoa Highway and in the town of Honomu, you can relax on the flats before starting on the second and final stage of the climb up Route 220, which is longer but not as steep.

At Akaka Falls Park, lock your bike at the parking lot, and take the short hike through the jungle to see Kahuna and Akaka Falls. Both waterfalls are impressive as they hurl water some 400 feet into small pools below.

The return trip to Hilo is a snap, but before getting back onto Hawaii Belt Road, be sure to stop in Honomu for lunch. And, yes, they do have ice cream, and by this point you will have earned it.

Flowing through Lava
The Puna District

Number of miles:	20.2
Approximate pedaling time:	3 hours
Terrain:	Rolling hills
Traffic:	Light
Things to see:	Geothermal plant, papaya farms, Isaac Hale Beach Park, lava flows, Lava Tree State Park
Food:	Snacks in Pahoa
Facilities:	Rest rooms and water in Pahoa

Puna is the name of the Big Island's easternmost district. This thinly populated region has seen quite a bit of volcanic activity in recent years, and riding here will take you through lava flows that have erased entire communities.

Before you start a ride in Puna, make sure you have a sturdy pair of wheels and a good set of spare tubes. Many of Puna's desolate roads are in disrepair, and the threat of future volcanic activity puts them at the bottom of the Department of Transportation's to-do list. And to increase your margin of safety, plan to tour Puna with a riding partner.

The ride starts in Pahoa, a gritty little town in the heart of Puna. From the Pahoa Neighborhood Facility, ride east onto Route 132 and into a tunnel of trees. These trees have capitalized on the region's abundant rainfall, building themselves into towering giants that darken the roads with their shadows.

At 3.2 miles, you veer to the right onto Pohoiki Road. The smooth pavement seems good at first, but the road quickly narrows to a single-car width and the surface becomes rough and

broken all the way to Isaac Hale Beach Park. This is where the sturdy wheels come in handy. On the way to the park you will pass a geothermal energy plant on your left. The plant had been widely criticized by area residents who objected to its location, noise, and foul odors, but plant operators claim it's helping to reduce Hawaii's dependence on imported oil.

Beyond the geothermal plant, look for papaya trees, also on your left. Puna produces 95 percent of the state's papayas. Puna's growers are now facing a big challenge. In 1992 some of their trees were struck by the papaya ringspot virus. Harmless to humans, the virus strikes at the papaya tree's ability to draw energy from the sun and causes the tree to die. University of Hawaii scientists made a breakthrough in their efforts to produce a genetically altered papaya that is resistant to the virus. The new variety still has to be approved by the government, but it's expected to be on the market in time to save the multimillion-dollar industry.

Isaac Hale Beach Park has a small boat ramp and a little harbor. Terrible road conditions persist as you ride past the park and up the coast. The surrounding vegetation is dense jungle with numerous pandanas trees growing near the road. At 9.4 miles into the ride, the road cuts through a lava flow, and suddenly you will find the landscape barren. For miles it's nothing but black rock stretching out far and wide.

The road widens and becomes smoother at this point, and soon you are zipping over what used to be the village of Kapoho. This settlement was wiped out in 1960 when Kilauea volcano erupted and sent a finger of lava down the coast. Although lava flows are common in Hawaii, it's rare that a person is killed by them. Scientists monitoring the volcano are quick to close roads that are in danger of being overrun.

On some of the older lava flows, white-colored lichens and moss are starting to form on the black rocks. This is nature's first step in colonizing the barren landscape. Next, it will be ferns, grass, and eventually trees. It takes a long time for the land to recover, but the abundant rainfall in Puna helps things along.

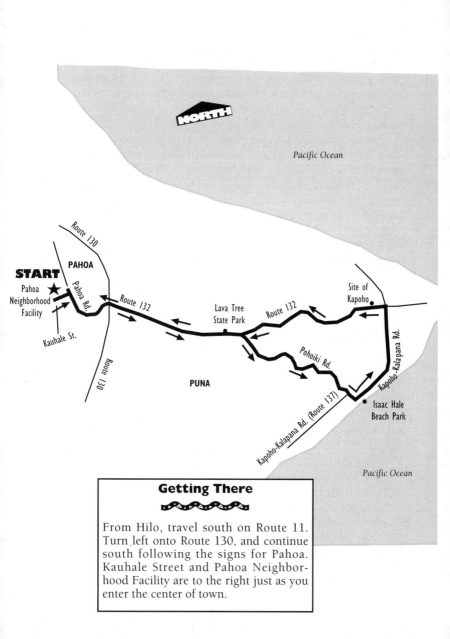

NORTH

Pacific Ocean

Route 130

PAHOA

START

Pahoa
Neighborhood
Facility

Pahoa Rd.

Route 132

Kauhale St.

Route 130

PUNA

Lava Tree
State Park

Route 132

Pohoiki Rd.

Kapoho-Kalapana Rd. (Route 137)

Site of
Kapoho

Kapoho-Kalapana Rd.

Isaac Hale
Beach Park

Pacific Ocean

Getting There

From Hilo, travel south on Route 11.
Turn left onto Route 130, and continue
south following the signs for Pahoa.
Kauhale Street and Pahoa Neighborhood Facility are to the right just as you
enter the center of town.

0.0 From Pahoa Neighborhood Facility, turn left onto Kauhale Street.

0.05 Turn right onto Pahoa Road.

0.4 After stopping at the sign, proceed straight across the intersection onto Route 132.

3.2 Veer right onto Pohoiki Road.

7.9 Turn left at Isaac Hale Beach Park onto Kapoho-Kalapana Road (Route 137).

11.7 Turn left onto Route 132.

19.8 After stopping at the sign, proceed straight across the intersection onto Pahoa Road.

20.2 Turn left onto Kauhale Street.

20.25 Turn right into Pahoa Neighborhood Facility.

There is a small shoulder along Route 132, and the trip back to Pahoa is slightly uphill. You will return to the tunnel of trees you passed through on the outbound ride, and you will see Lava Tree State Park on your right. The park features rock columns, or chimneys, that formed as lava poured through the area and cooled around tree trunks. It takes only a few minutes to walk the narrow asphalt trail through the park, and soon you will be back on your way to Pahoa.

The Wrath of Pele
South of Pahoa

Number of miles:	27.7 miles
Approximate pedaling time:	4 hours
Terrain:	Rolling hills
Traffic:	Light
Things to see:	Jungles, a black-sand beach, cooled lava flows, Star of the Sea painted church
Food:	Snacks in Pahoa
Facilities:	Rest rooms and water in Pahoa

Pele shows little mercy when she decides to expand the Big Island. In 1990 she covered the town of Kalapana with molten rock, leaving behind scarcely a trace of this once vibrant community. But residents of the Puna region have long known it's futile to argue with the goddess of fire. They just try to stay out of her way.

Economically, this area is not well off. Major businesses and hotels are reluctant to commit resources here because of the volcanic activity. Consequently, the area is wonderfully undeveloped, and it attracts the kind of people who are flexible enough to live around molten lava. The landscape consists of green jungles streaked with stark, barren lava flows.

Riding in this area requires sturdy wheels and tires. Many of Puna's roads are paved but badly in need of repair. Kapoho-Kalapana Road (Route 137) and Kamaili Road are two such examples. For an added level of safety, plan to ride with a friend, and as usual carry spare tubes and patch kits.

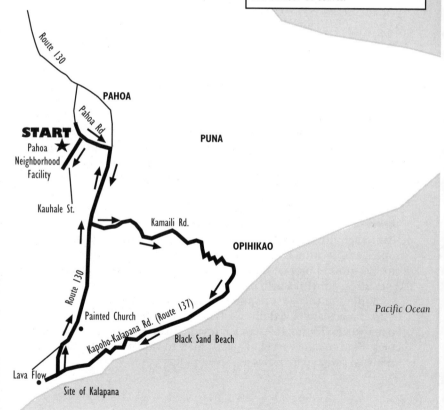

NORTH

Getting There

From Hilo, travel south on Route 11. Turn left onto Route 130, and continue south following the signs for Pahoa. Kauhale Street and Pahoa Neighorhood Facility are to the right just as you enter the center of town.

Route 130

PAHOA

Pahoa Rd.

START
Pahoa Neighborhood Facility

PUNA

Kauhale St.

Kamaili Rd.

OPIHIKAO

Route 130

Painted Church

Kapoho-Kalapana Rd. (Route 137)

Pacific Ocean

Black Sand Beach

Lava Flow

Site of Kalapana

DIREC-TIONS at a glance

0.0	From Pahoa Neighborhood Facility, turn left onto Kauhale Street.
0.05	Turn right onto Pahoa Road.
0.4	Turn right onto Route 130.
4.4	At the sign for Opihikao, turn left onto Kamaili Road.
9.7	Turn right onto Kapoho-Kalapana Road (Route 137).
17.6	Turn around where Kapoho-Kalapana Road (Route 137) has been covered with lava.
17.9	Turn left, staying on Kapoho-Kalapana Road (Route 137). This road connects with Route 130.
18.4	Turn right onto Route 130.
27.3	Turn left onto Pahoa Road.
27.7	Turn left onto Kauhale Street.
27.75	Return to Pahoa Neighborhood Facility.

To see Pele's handiwork, start your ride in the town of Pahoa at the Pahoa Neighborhood Facility. The attitude in this town is casual, and the people here are open-minded. Walking around barefoot and pursuing the hippie lifestyle is common. Small wooden buildings line either side of Pahoa Road, and cars slow to a crawl as drivers forage for parking spaces.

Once on Route 130, you will be on smooth open pavement as you leave the town behind and begin to ride rolling hills toward the coast. After a scenic viewpoint, you will turn left on Kamaili Road, at a sign that directs you to Opihikao.

Kamaili Road plunges down a very steep hill, but it eventually flattens out and becomes narrow as it passes houses and papaya farms. As you proceed down this road, the jungle thickens and the pavement becomes worse. This is about as far off the beaten path as you can get in Hawaii. Any farther into the wilderness and you would need a mountain bike. During the weekends it's likely you will see other vehicles on the road as people go to the shore to fish or swim, but during the weekdays, these jungle roads are quiet.

Turn right onto Kapoho-Kalapana Road (Route 137), named for the two communities it once connected. Both of the villages, however, have since been destroyed by lava. As you head down the coast to where Kalapana used to be, you will pass a few homes, and you will emerge from the shade of the jungle into the sunlight.

At 13.5 miles into the day's ride, a viewpoint will appear on your left. Before the viewpoint is a trail on the side of the road that leads down to a small black-sand beach. For some people the beach is clothing-optional.

A short distance after the viewpoint, the pavement gets better, and you are faced with a series of tiny hills that turn the road into a mini roller coaster. The hills are fun at first, but they wear you out quickly.

Finally you reach the point where lava covers the road. There is something sobering about this sight. Perhaps it's because you feel the eternity of geologic time. How many years will it be before this land is covered with trees again? What will this place look like in ten, fifty, or a hundred years from now? And what about the coconut trees, black-sand beach, and the 165 houses of Kalapana? Now that they have been buried in lava, it's as if they never existed.

After you turn around here and ride up to Route 130, you may be surprised to find that Kalapana has a survivor. Look for the Star of the Sea painted church, on your right. Before it could be gobbled up by lava, the church was picked up and moved from Kalapana to its new location. The church's interior is painted with colorful murals.

The ride back to Pahoa on Route 130 is uphill most of the way. The climb will give you plenty of time to decide whether you have what it takes to live next to a volcano.

To the Volcano
Hawaii Volcanoes National Park

Number of miles:	18.8
Approximate pedaling time:	2 hours
Terrain:	Hill
Traffic:	Moderate
Things to see:	Hawaii Volcanoes National Park
Food:	Snacks at Hirano Store, meals at Volcano House
Facilities:	Rest rooms and water at Glenwood Park and volcano visitor center

Visiting Hawaii Volcanoes National Park is a must, in order to see Kilauea, Hawaii's very active volcano. The Hawaii Belt Road (Route 11) will take you directly from sea level in Hilo to an elevation of almost 4,000 feet at the park, in a distance of 28 miles. Some cyclists rush to do this climb, only to find they have run out of energy by the time they reach the park entrance.

If you want to have enough energy to explore the park after you get there (see ride No. 34), and if the daunting task of starting from Hilo seems too much, try the ride described here by starting farther up the road, at Glenwood Park, 18.8 miles from Hilo. (Glenwood Park is situated before the intersection of Glenwood Road and the Hawaii Belt Road. Ignore maps that incorrectly indicate that the park is at the intersection.) Hirano Store is conveniently located right across the street from the small park.

The ride immediately begins uphill on Hawaii Belt Road. Glenwood Park is at an elevation near 2,300 feet, so it's 9.2 miles and 1,680 feet of climbing until you reach the national

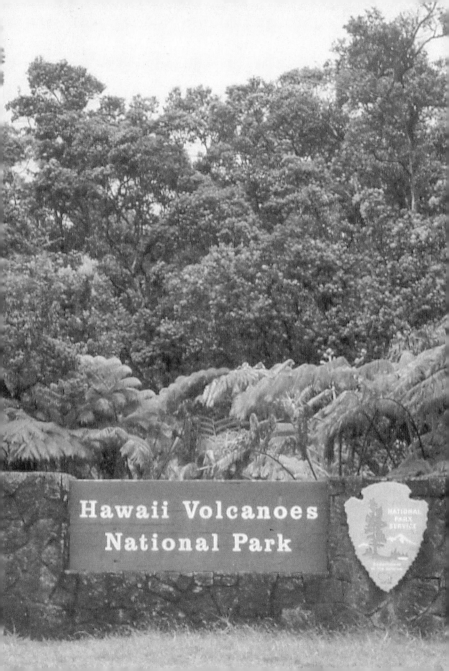

park. Heading upward, you are aided by a northeasterly tail-wind. It's an unusual feeling to have the wind blow you uphill, but you learn to appreciate it very quickly.

The first mile of the ride is the most difficult. Rough shoulders exist on the roadway, but they gradually improve as the road becomes less steep and you near the town of Volcano.

From Glenwood to the national park, the countryside is lush and green. As you gain in altitude you will begin to notice the air becoming crisp and cool. By the time you reach the town of Volcano the clouds hover close, and it's common to smell wood burning in people's fireplaces. You might want to bring a jacket because the weather changes quickly at the upper elevations.

This area receives about 100 inches of rainfall a year, and plants grow quickly. Inside the national park a great deal of effort is made to keep aggressive foreign plants out. Fences prevent wild pigs from coming into the park and damaging delicate plants or spreading weed seeds. Outside the park, however, Hawaiian trees like the ohia lehua have to battle it out.

As you approach the entrance to the national park, the road's shoulders disappear. A left turn brings you to the guard shack where you pay your entrance fee. The nice thing is that bikes are charged less than cars.

A great place to see Kilauea Crater is from the Volcano House restaurant, on your left just after the visitor center. From the restaurant, a spectacular view of the crater stretches out before you. It's also a good spot for enjoying a snack before you head back down the mountain or continue exploring the crater (see ride No. 34).

The return trip on Hawaii Belt Road is a curious affair. The tailwind you had earlier is now a headwind, and it acts against you like an air brake. Luckily, gravity prevails, and your weight comes in handy for once. Before you know it you will be coasting down the mountain.

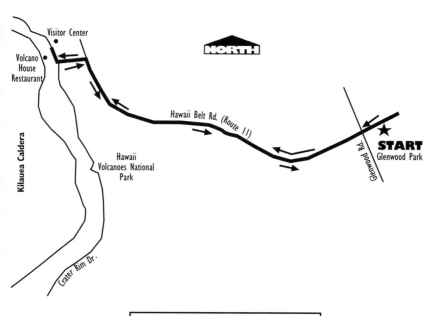

Getting There

From Hilo, travel southwest on Hawaii Belt Road (Route 11). Glenwood Park is on the left at 18.8 miles, across from Hirano Store and before you reach the intersection of Glenwood Road.

DIREC-TIONS at a glance

0.0   From Glenwood Park, turn left onto Hawaii Belt Road (Route 11), and ride west.

9.2   Turn left into Hawaii Volcanoes National Park.

9.4   Turn around at the visitor center and leave the park by the way you came in (see ride No. 34 for tour of the crater rim).

9.6   Turn right onto Hawaii Belt Road (Route 11).

18.8   Turn right into Glenwood Park.

34 Into the Volcano
Kilauea Caldera

Number of miles:	10.7 miles
Approximate pedaling time:	1.5 hours
Terrain:	Rolling hills
Traffic:	Light
Things to see:	Kilauea Caldera, Halemaumau Crater, ohia lehua forest, cooled lava flows
Food:	Snacks and meals at Volcano House
Facilities:	Rest rooms and water at visitor center

Perched at 3,980 feet above sea level, the Kilauea volcano at Hawaii Volcanoes National Park attracts thousands of visitors every year. Kilauea keeps scientists busy trying to understand the great natural forces at work. It is the most active volcano in the world. Most people tour the volcano in a bus or a car, but to really feel the spirit of Pele, goddess of fire, nothing beats a bicycle.

Start at the visitor center, and after checking out the displays, roll out to Crater Rim Drive. This road will take you around the volcano and close to Halemaumau Crater, a smaller crater within the large caldera (main crater).

The sights begin only two-tenths of a mile from the visitor center, with sulfur vents on the right. Here the ground is stained yellow as puffs of gas and steam belch smelly sulfur out of the ground.

At eight-tenths of a mile, you will see two steam vents on the left. The steam is caused when rainwater seeps into cracks in the earth and becomes heated by the volcano. The landscape on this part of the ride is dotted with a thinned-out ohia lehua forest. The trees are easy to spot with their delicate, spiny, red flowers. To see into the caldera itself, stop at the Kilauea Overlook on your left.

At the Jaggar Museum, check out the cool displays, including a seismic sensor like the ones used to measure earthquakes. You are invited to stomp on the ground and watch the needle go wild as it measures the vibration. You can also watch videos about the volcano.

Outside the museum the view of the volcano below will amaze you, not only by its size but by its complexity. Smaller craters exist within the large caldera, and recent lava flows cross over fissures and older lava flows.

From the museum, Crater Rim Drive winds down a fast descent to the floor of the caldera. The landscape inside the caldera is barren, with black lava flows. There are two types of lava. See if you can tell the difference between the smooth, billowy *pahoehoe* flows and the rough, crumbly flows of *aa* (pronounced AH-ah).

Inside the caldera you are likely to feel the full effects of the trade winds as they blow over the northeast rim and sweep across the lower southwest sections. These winds will make the flat road to Halemaumau Crater difficult. From the Halemaumau parking lot, you can take a quick walk to see into the crater. Older people, children, pregnant women, and anyone else who might be sensitive to strong sulfur dioxide fumes should avoid this stop.

Halemaumau Crater is 280 feet deep and nearly 3,000 feet across. It erupted spectacularly in 1924 and in 1967-1968. Since then, during lesser eruptions, the level of the lava lake inside the crater has fluctuated, periodically rising above the rim and sending flows out into the caldera.

From the lower section of the caldera, Crater Rim Drive goes uphill to the northeastern rim. Expect headwinds the whole way, until you get into a forest of ohia lehua and ferns. The ohia lehua is common here but is becoming increasingly rare elsewhere in the Hawaiian Islands. This area represents what a Hawaiian rain forest looked like before the introduction of aggressive foreign plants.

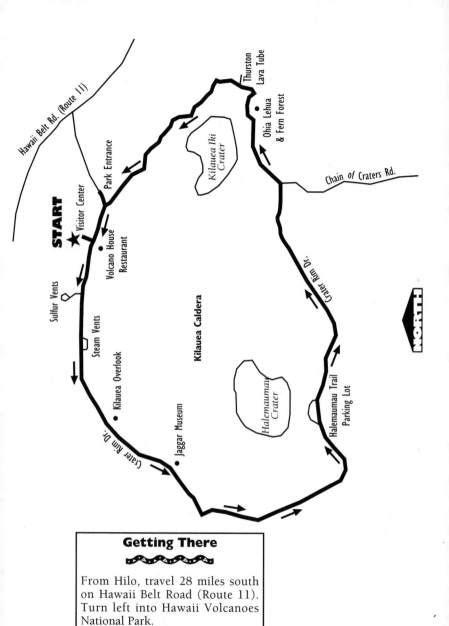

Thurston Lava Tube

Ohia Lehua & Fern Forest

Hawaii Belt Rd. (Route 11)

Park Entrance

Chain of Craters Rd.

START

Visitor Center

Kilauea Iki Crater

Volcano House Restaurant

Kilauea Caldera

Sulfur Vents

Crater Rim Dr.

Steam Vents

Kilauea Overlook

Halemaumau Crater

Halemaumau Trail Parking Lot

NORTH

Jaggar Museum

Crater Rim Dr.

Getting There

From Hilo, travel 28 miles south on Hawaii Belt Road (Route 11). Turn left into Hawaii Volcanoes National Park.

DIREC-TIONS at a glance

0.0   From the visitor center, turn right onto Crater Rim Drive.

10.6   Turn left, staying on Crater Rim Drive.

10.7   Turn right into the visitor center.

The next major attraction is the Thurston Lava Tube, formed about 350 to 500 years ago when an eruption ended and the lava drained away. Get off your bike to walk through the dark tunnel that drips with rainwater from the ceiling. Crater Rim Drive finally takes you downhill past Kilauea Iki Crater and back to the visitor center.

Flying High
Mauna Loa Road

Number of miles:	20.4
Approximate pedaling time:	3 hours
Terrain:	Hill
Traffic:	Light
Things to see:	Wild pheasants, Keamoku lava flow, Kipuka Ki Special Ecological Area
Food:	Snacks at nearby town of Volcano
Facilities:	None

There are only a few roads in this world that inspire us to become hill climbers, and Mauna Loa Road is one them. No matter how much you hate fighting gravity, this road spurs you on until you reach the top.

Begin your ride at the Bird Park, just 1.5 miles off Hawaii Belt Road (Route 11). From 4,000 feet above sea level, the road starts off being wide enough for two-way traffic. But after 2.5 miles, it narrows to a one-car width and remains that way to the top of the road at an elevation of 6,660 feet. The good news is that the road is so curvy that cars are forced to go slow—and because this is a dead-end road, there are very few cars to begin with.

The pavement at first is smooth, but tree roots have lifted the asphalt in some places. The result is smooth sections interrupted by patches of bumps. You hardly notice this until you make the trip down and find yourself gripping the brakes hard to keep from taking the bumps too fast. Mountain bikes will have no problem, but for added safety, road bikes should be outfitted with wide, sturdy tires.

The forest lining the road starts off with tall trees, but as you continue up the slope, the trees diminish in height, and soon you are in the open. The weather is cool at this elevation, and the road is subject to quickly changing weather conditions. On cloudy days this road becomes obscured by mist, and you can imagine you are climbing toward an alpine mountain pass in the Tour de France. On clear days the sun shines, though, and there's nothing but blue skies and the winding road.

If you are riding in the early morning or late afternoon, you will see many wild pheasants and other birds that forage near the road. The Bird Park, also called Kipuka Puaulu, and the Kipuka Ki Special Ecological Area are within the boundaries of Hawaii Volcanoes National Park. A "kipuka" is an old vegetated lava flow that is surrounded by newer flows. The plants and animals within this area are protected. Perhaps the birds know this, because they allow you to come very close before they dash into the bushes.

At one point, Mauna Loa Road cuts through a section of the Keamoku lava flow. The black crumbly rock serves to remind you that Mauna Loa, the mountain you are climbing, is an active volcano. Mauna Loa is the second-highest mountain in the state, at 13,679 feet. (The highest is Mauna Kea at 13,796 feet, also on the Big Island.) Over the years, eruptions on Mauna Loa have been slowing down. The last eruption was in 1984, and it was relatively short-lived. But Mauna Loa has erupted thirty-three times within the last 150 years, and there is little doubt it will erupt again. The only question is when.

An eruption usually is preceded by two observations. The first is inflation of the summit of the volcano, and the second is an increased level of seismic activity. Since the 1984 eruption, scientists have been measuring the mountain's rate of deformation, and they believe that the summit of Mauna Loa is indeed inflating with magma. But the rate of seismic activity has been relatively low, so the next eruption could be a few years off.

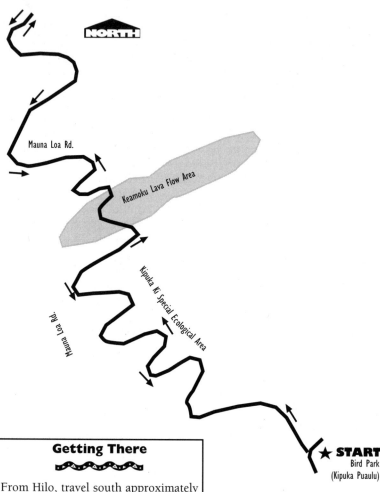

NORTH

Mauna Loa Rd.

Keamoku Lava Flow Area

Kipuka Kī Special Ecological Area

Mauna Loa Rd.

Getting There

From Hilo, travel south approximately
30 miles on Hawaii Belt Road (Route
11), passing the entrance to Hawaii
Volcanoes National Park. Turn right
onto Mauna Loa Road, and travel 1.5
miles to the parking area at the Bird
Park (Kipuka Puaulu).

★ **START**
Bird Park
(Kipuka Puaulu)

DIREC-TIONS at a glance

0.0 From the parking area at the Bird Park, ride uphill on Mauna Loa Road.

10.2 Turn around at the top, and retrace your route down the mountain.

20.4 Return to the Bird Park.

At the top of Mauna Loa Road, you have to turn around and roll down the mountain. Even if you hate climbing, you'll want to return again to ascend this road because of the clean air, the lack of traffic, and the wild birds.

Place of Refuge
South of Kealakekua

Number of miles:	11.2
Approximate pedaling time:	1.5 hours
Terrain:	Hills
Traffic:	Light
Things to see:	Kealakekua Bay, St. Benedict's painted church, Puuhonua o Honaunau National Historical Park
Food:	Snacks at the coffee mill and at the town of Captain Cook
Facilities:	Rest rooms and water at Puuhonua o Honaunau National Historical Park

Before the arrival of Captain Cook in 1778, Hawaiians lived by sacred rules of life called *kapu.* These rules governed every aspect of day-to-day life and ensured respect for the *alii,* or chiefs.

The kapu made it forbidden to touch the alii's possessions or to let your shadow fall on the chief's palace grounds. There were rules on what kinds of fish could be caught during the year, where you could fish, and who could eat the fish. The rules established order within society, and they served as a conservation policy that ensured a stable supply of food and materials.

The Hawaiians had only one punishment for breaking a kapu, and that punishment was death. The only way to avoid this punishment was to retreat to a place of refuge such as Puuhonua o Honaunau.

The ride to this place starts at Kealakekua Bay, where Captain Cook was killed in 1779. From the rocky coast, pedal uphill on Napoopoo Road, which makes its way past small rural homes and a coffee mill. The roadway is narrow, and on weekends it's busy with tourists and beachgoers.

It's quieter once you turn onto Middle Keei Road, where you will be treated to the sweet smell of the plumeria blossoms that grow along the road. This small road continues uphill, lined with modest homes. The residents of this area have green yards that grow wild with coconut trees, bougainvillea, and ti plants.

On Painted Church Road, you will experience a slight downhill section as you pass through similar neighborhoods. The road is named after St. Benedict's painted church, famous for its interior murals and frescoes. A sign directs you to the church on the left. The church with its elaborate steeple stands out brightly against blue skies and the green southwest slopes of Mauna Loa. Surrounding the church is a small graveyard ringed with colorful flowers.

When you are done exploring the church, begin your fast downhill ride on Ke Ala Keawe Road (Route 160), and then turn left into Puuhonua o Honaunau National Historical Park.

After you lock your bike up and pay the entrance fee, take a walking tour. In ancient Hawaii, Honaunau was divided, with the refuge being on the point nearest the ocean and the palace grounds of the alii being farther inland. A large rock wall, built in the late 1500s, separates the two areas. The Hawaiians made it by fitting stones together without the use of concrete or mortar.

Hale o Keawe Heiau stands on the border between the palace grounds and the refuge and is the most prominent feature of the park. The heiau, or temple, served as a place to store the bones of the chiefs. The bones were believed to have great spiritual power, or mana.

In the refuge itself you will find many coconut trees and two stone foundations of other heiaus. A person who broke a kapu could expect to stay in the refuge for a short time after a priest performed a ceremony of absolution. In addition to people who broke the kapu, defeated soldiers or women and children seek-

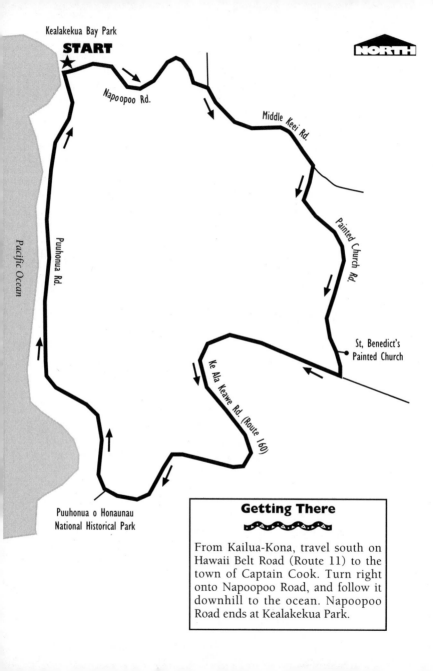

Kealakekua Bay Park
START

Napoopoo Rd.

Middle Keei Rd.

NORTH

Painted Church Rd.

St, Benedict's
Painted Church

Pacific Ocean

Puuhonua Rd.

Ke Ala Keawe Rd. (Route 160)

Puuhonua o Honaunau
National Historical Park

Getting There

From Kailua-Kona, travel south on Hawaii Belt Road (Route 11) to the town of Captain Cook. Turn right onto Napoopoo Road, and follow it downhill to the ocean. Napoopoo Road ends at Kealakekua Park.

DIREC-TIONS
at a glance

0.0 From Kealakekua Bay Park, ride uphill on Napoopoo Road.

1.7 Turn right onto Middle Keei Road.

2.5 Turn right onto Painted Church Road.

4.6 Turn right onto Ke Ala Keawe Road (Route 160).

7.0 Turn left into Puuhonua o Honaunau National Historical Park.

7.1 Turn around at the park and leave by the way you came in.

7.2 Turn left onto Puuhonua Road

11.2 Return to Kealakekua Bay Park.

ing protection in times of war could come to the safety of the refuge. The difficult part of seeking refuge was getting to the Puuhonua. Because it was cut off from the rest of the island by the Allii's land, one had to swim to the refuge from across the bay.

At the park you may see Hawaiians continuing the ancient craft of weaving pandanas leaves together to make beautiful mats. The leaves undergo a great deal of preparation before they can be used. Some projects require the leaves to soak in the ocean for as long as a month.

Return to Kealakekua Bay by taking a left turn from the refuge park onto Puuhonua Road. The sunshine is intense on this stretch of the ride, and the road is narrow. Luckily, the terrain is flat, and you return to Kealakekua Bay in just 4 short miles.

Kamehameha Kona Cruise
South of Kailua-Kona

Number of miles:	15.4
Approximate pedaling time:	1.5 hours
Terrain:	Mostly flat
Traffic:	Heavy on Alii Drive
Things to see:	Downtown Kailua-Kona, Ahuena Heiau, Kuamoo battleground
Food:	Meals and snacks in downtown Kailua-Kona and Keauhou Shopping Village
Facilities:	Rest rooms and water at Old Kona Airport Park

King Kamehameha could have lived anywhere he wanted after he conquered the Hawaiian Islands, but he decided to return to the Big Island to retire in the Kona district. Located on the west side of Hawaii, between Hualalai and Mauna Loa, Kona is one of the few places that is protected from the northeasterly trade winds. Time seems to stop in the Kona area, where there's little seasonal variation in the weather, and one sunny day seems to blur into the next.

Alii Drive in the town of Kailua-Kona is the epicenter of activity for this growing tourist destination, and it's beginning to take on the flavor of Waikiki. The ride starts at the Old Kona Airport Park and heads south through the heart of downtown Kailua-Kona. When you turn onto Alii Drive, expect to find a lot of traffic.

The road surface is rough at first, but it gets smoother as you head south. In some places the road has nice shoulders, but beachgoers tend to use them for parking. On weekends the beaches are brimming with activity as people get outside to enjoy the sun and surf.

The first point of interest is Kamehameha's home, called Kamakahonu. Lock your bike at the pier and walk to the house that Kamehameha built, and check out the nearby Ahuena Heiau, or temple.

The grass-roof structure of the living quarters and the heiau makes it easy to imagine what the area was like before development. From his home, Kamehameha must have been able to see the entire coastline with its coconut trees, small beaches, and rocky outcrops. Probably the biggest difference between then and now is the sight of hotels. One hotel sits right next to Kamehameha's home, and several others have been built along the coast.

Mokuaikaua Church also changed the landscape when it was built in 1837. This first Christian church in Hawaii stands out prominently above the coast as you look from Kamehameha's home.

Continue riding on Alii Drive, passing a concrete seawall and various tourist shops. Alii Drive leads to Alii Highway, but before you get there you have to climb a short hill. With the hill out of the way, smooth pavement takes you to where the road comes to a dead end.

Near this area is the Kuamoo battleground where King Kamehameha's nephew died as he tried to defend the ancient kapu system. This system defined daily life for the Hawaiians, and breaking the kapu could mean death. While Kamehameha was alive, he kept the kapu intact. But when he died, the old belief system came under attack by ideas introduced by Western sailors and missionaries. Eventually the kapu system was abandoned.

On the way back to the Old Kona Airport Park, you can pretend you are finishing the Ironman Triathlon World Championship. The triathlon was created in Hawaii, and over the years it became famous for ending here on Alii Drive. After swimming for 2 miles, cycling for 100 miles, and running a complete marathon, competitors were welcomed by huge crowds as they jogged their final steps down this road.

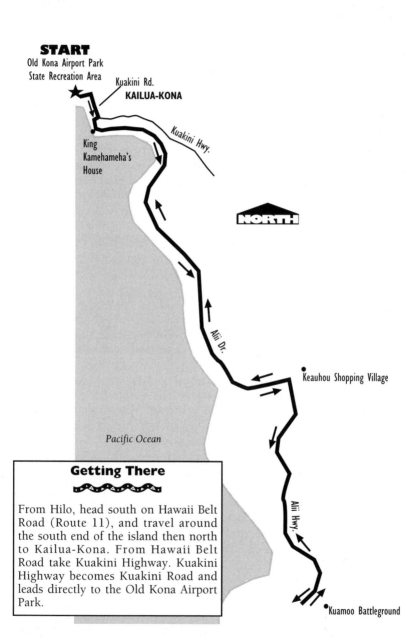

START
Old Kona Airport Park
State Recreation Area

Kuakini Rd.
KAILUA-KONA

Kuakini Hwy.

King
Kamehameha's
House

NORTH

Alii Dr.

Keauhou Shopping Village

Pacific Ocean

Alii Hwy.

Kuamoo Battleground

Getting There

From Hilo, head south on Hawaii Belt
Road (Route 11), and travel around
the south end of the island then north
to Kailua-Kona. From Hawaii Belt
Road take Kuakini Highway. Kuakini
Highway becomes Kuakini Road and
leads directly to the Old Kona Airport
Park.

DIREC-TIONS at a glance

0.0 From Old Kona Airport Park, turn right onto Kuakini Road.
0.6 Turn right onto Alii Drive.
6.2 Turn right onto Alii Highway.
7.7 Turn around at the end of Alii Highway and retrace your route to Alii Drive.
9.2 Turn left onto Alii Drive.
14.8 Turn left onto Kuakini Road.
15.4 Turn left into Old Kona Airport Park.

Petroglyph Puzzle
Puako

Number of miles:	12.3
Approximate pedaling time:	1.5 hours
Terrain:	Mostly flat
Traffic:	Heavy on Queen Kaahumanu Highway (Route 19)
Things to see:	Mountain views, ancient petroglyphs
Food:	Snacks and meals at Waikoloa Beach Resort at the King's Shops
Facilities:	Rest rooms and water at Anaehoomalu and Holoholokai beach parks

To see the largest concentration of petroglyphs in Hawaii, take a trip to Puako Petroglyph Archaeological Preserve, in the South Kohala district.

Start the ride at Anaehoomalu Beach Park, situated next to Waikoloa Beach Resort. The Waikoloa Resort and its neighbor up the road, the Mauna Lani Resort, are expensive establishments near the sea. They have no problem attracting tourists to South Kohala, where it's bright and sunny all year long. The resorts and their surrounding golf courses were built on barren lava fields, which extend far up-slope to the vent of the Mauna Kea volcano. During the day, the dark lava rocks are heated by the sun until you imagine them becoming molten again.

After you leave Anaehoomalu Beach Park, head toward Queen Kaahumanu Highway (Route 19), where you begin a short northward journey to Mauna Lani Resort. The highway that you ride is part of the course for the Ironman Triathlon World Championship. Here it's common to see cyclists hunched over high-tech,

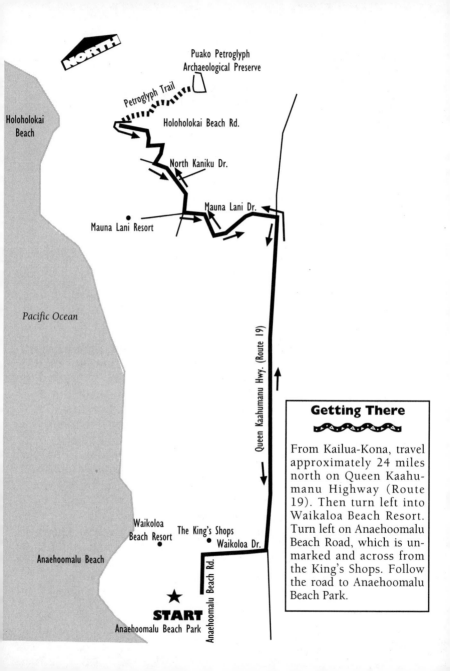

NORTH

Puako Petroglyph
Archaeological Preserve

Petroglyph Trail

Holoholokai Beach Rd.

Holoholokai
Beach

North Kaniku Dr.

Mauna Lani Dr.

Mauna Lani Resort

Pacific Ocean

Queen Kaahumanu Hwy. (Route 19)

Waikoloa
Beach Resort

The King's Shops

Waikoloa Dr.

Anaehoomalu Beach

Anaehoomalu Beach Rd.

★
START
Anaehoomalu Beach Park

Getting There

From Kailua-Kona, travel approximately 24 miles north on Queen Kaahumanu Highway (Route 19). Then turn left into Waikaloa Beach Resort. Turn left on Anaehoomalu Beach Road, which is unmarked and across from the King's Shops. Follow the road to Anaehoomalu Beach Park.

DIREC-TIONS at a glance

0.0 From Anaehoomalu Beach Park, exit onto Anaehoomalu Beach Road.

0.3 Turn right onto Waikoloa Drive.

0.9 Turn left onto Queen Kaahumanu Highway (Route 19).

3.5 Turn left onto Mauna Lani Drive.

4.6 At the traffic circle, turn right onto North Kaniku Drive, and follow the signs for Puako Petroglyph Park.

5.5 At the sign for Puako Petroglyph Archaeological Preserve, turn right onto Holoholokai Beach Road.

6.0 Turn around at Puako Petroglyph Archaeological Preserve, and retrace your route on Holoholokai Beach Road.

6.5 Turn left onto North Kaniku Drive.

7.4 At the traffic circle follow the signs for Queen Kaahumanu Highway (Route 19).

8.5 Turn right onto Queen Kaahumanu Highway (Route 19).

11.1 Turn right onto Waikoloa Drive.

12.0 Turn left onto Anaehoomalu Beach Road.

12.3 Return to Anaehoomalu Beach Park.

aerodynamic bicycles, training for the day they will push their bodies to the limit. It's hard to appreciate what they are trying to do until you get out there and try it for yourself.

The first thing that impresses you once you get on the highway is the wind. Funneled between Mauna Kea and the Kohala Mountains, the trades whip past you and create a deafening roar as they try to knock you off your bike. There is no vegetation or any sort of natural barrier to protect you from the gusting winds. Triathletes endure hours of this kind of training, but you have to ride the highway for only 2.6 miles until you turn left onto Mauna Lani Drive.

The drive takes you to Mauna Lani Resort through sharp, lava-rock dunes. Clearly marked signs then make it easy to find your way to Holoholokai Beach Park and to the nearby petroglyph preserve.

The first petroglyphs you see are reproductions near the trail head. With rice paper, you can make etchings of these reproductions. The original petroglyphs, however, are delicate and should not be disturbed in this way. To see them, lock your bike up and take a 15-minute walk through a thicket of kiawe trees.

The shady kiawe trees were introduced after Captain Cook's discovery of the islands, so they were not around at the time the petroglyphs were carved. The Hawaiians who made these images must have used something to shade themselves from the intense sun, or perhaps they worked on them in the early morning or late afternoon.

The petroglyphs, very simple and elegant human figures, are spread over a large slab of reddish-brown rock. What the petroglyphs are trying to convey and why they were made is something that still puzzles archaeologists. As you look at these marks in the stone, your mind wanders back to the time when there were no hotels, no highway, no fluorescent-green golf courses, and no trees.

The return trip to Anaehoomalu Beach Park is marked by one significant challenge just as you leave Mauna Lani Drive and turn onto Queen Kaahumanu Highway. The wind seems to pick up at this point, and you have to be patient as you stagger through the powerful gusts in your easiest gear. Once down the highway, however, the going gets better.

From the open highway you can see the major mountains on Hawaii, from Kohala in the north to the twin giants of Mauna Kea and Mauna Loa and onto Hualalai in the south. The view of these mountains adds to the power and spirit of South Kohala, and perhaps it was this view that inspired the petroglyph carvers.

Smooth Sailing
Kapaau to Pololu Valley

Number of miles:	14.2
Approximate pedaling time:	2.5 hours
Terrain:	Rolling hills
Traffic:	Light
Things to see:	Original King Kamehameha statue, Pololu Valley Lookout, Keokea Beach Park
Food:	Snacks in Kapaau and nearby Hawi
Facilities:	Rest rooms and water at Kamehameha Park

The North Kohala district is where King Kamehameha was born, and it was from this part of Hawaii that he began his conquest of the Hawaiian Islands. When it was over, Kamehameha had unified the islands under one rule.

The ride in this region begins at Kamehameha Park in the small town of Kapaau and heads east to the Pololu Valley Lookout. Kapaau is a sedate little town, but in ancient times it must have been wild because it served as a place for fighting, dancing, sports, and games.

When you turn from the park onto Route 270, smooth pavement takes you through Kapaau and past a statue of King Kamehameha. This statue was salvaged from the sea after a shipping accident. Before this original was recovered, a copy was made to replace it, and now there are two statues. The copy stands in downtown Honolulu across from Iolani Palace.

Once past the town, continue east toward Pololu Valley. The roadway is smooth all the way, but at 2.6 miles it becomes narrow as it twists and turns uphill to the lookout. You have to

cross three narrow bridges before you get to the end of the road, but the road is not busy, and the bridges are very short.

In the past, this area was used to grow sugarcane, but that industry is long gone, and the economy has shifted toward tourism and ranching. Plants get plenty of rain and sunshine on this part of the island, and people put their gardens to good use. Some enterprising residents have roadside stands that depend on the honor system to sell macadamia nuts, tropical flowers, and fruits. The old values of honesty and trust are still very much alive here.

When you reach the lookout, you will see a spectacular view of Pololu Valley. The lookout is on a ledge, and the steep drop gives way to a view of the ocean and to Pololu's black-sand beach. Pololu Valley was formed when Kohala, the shield volcano that makes up this part of the island, experienced a catastrophic landslide more than 370,000 years ago. The slide opened up scars on the volcano that eventually became valleys, including this valley and Waipio Valley (see ride No. 40), 10 miles farther down the coast.

Pololu Valley has a lake and marsh system behind a large dune of black sand. The dune, kept in place by ironwood trees, separates lake from sea. The dune and lake were formed by the tsunami of 1946, according to some longtime Kohala residents, and core samples of the valley's soil seem to support this idea.

On your way back to Kapaau, take a break at Keokea Beach Park. The smooth road to the park is downhill, and the park is a great place to relax and watch waves explode along the rugged coast. The only drawback is the steep climb out of the park and back to Route 270. But once that is out of the way, the ride to Kapaau is quite easygoing.

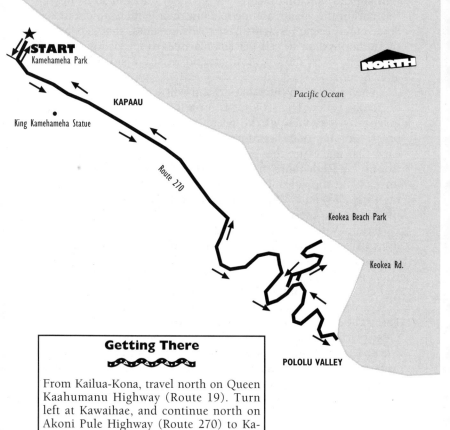

★ **START**
Kamehameha Park

NORTH

Pacific Ocean

KAPAAU

King Kamehameha Statue

Route 270

Keokea Beach Park

Keokea Rd.

POLOLU VALLEY

Getting There

From Kailua-Kona, travel north on Queen Kaahumanu Highway (Route 19). Turn left at Kawaihae, and continue north on Akoni Pule Highway (Route 270) to Kapaau. Kamehameha Park is on the left just before you enter Kapaau.

DIREC-TIONS at a glance

0.0 Start near the rest rooms at Kamehameha Park, and ride to the park's exit.

0.2 Turn left from the park onto Route 270, and ride east.

6.0 Turn around at Pololu Valley Lookout.

7.7 Turn right onto Keokea Road.

8.7 Turn around at Keokea Beach Park, and retrace your way back to Route 270.

9.8 Turn right onto Route 270.

14.0 Turn right into Kamehameha Park.

14.2 Return to starting point near rest rooms.

A Ride into the Past
Honokaa to Waipio Valley

Number of miles:	17.4
Approximate pedaling time:	2.5 hours
Terrain:	Rolling hills
Traffic:	Light
Things to see:	Waipio Valley, black-sand beach
Food:	Snacks and meals in Honokaa
Facilities:	Rest rooms and water at Honokaa Park

Visiting Honokaa is like going back in time. This little town, 39 miles north of Hilo, was created around the activities of a sugar plantation. Since the plantation closed down, the fields have either been put to other uses or are being overrun by weeds. But the people who worked on the plantation remain.

Start the ride at Honokaa Park, and take your time checking out the small shops on Mamane Street. You will find the town has not been homogenized with franchised chain stores. Here you have establishments like Herb's Place, S. Hasegawa Ltd., and Tex Drive In—a refreshing change from Burger King, Kmart, and McDonald's.

Honokaa sits on huge sea cliffs that overlook the Pacific Ocean, and the town catches the best of the northeasterly trade winds. From here it's just 8.7 miles down the road to the scenic lookout at Waipio Valley. The gentle downhill ride to Waipio Valley is fairly easy. After you leave the town behind you, Mamane Street passes by a few small homes that are built down from the road. Being on the windward side of the island, this region benefits from abundant rainfall, and the countryside is green and grassy.

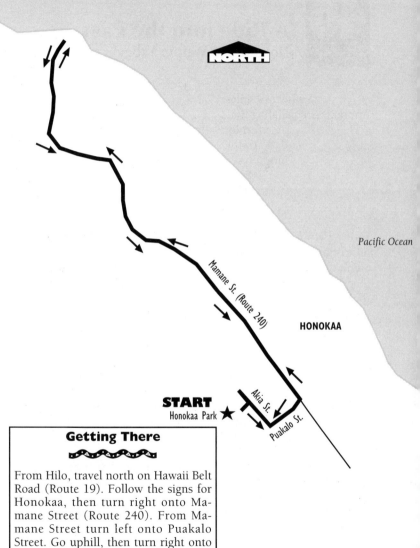

Waipio Bay

NORTH

Pacific Ocean

Mamane St. (Route 240)

HONOKAA

START
Honokaa Park ★

Akia St.

Puakalo St.

Getting There

From Hilo, travel north on Hawaii Belt Road (Route 19). Follow the signs for Honokaa, then turn right onto Mamane Street (Route 240). From Mamane Street turn left onto Puakalo Street. Go uphill, then turn right onto Akia Street. Honokaa Park is to your left.

DIREC-TIONS at a glance

0.0 From Honokaa Park, turn right onto Akia Street.

0.05 Turn left onto Puakalo Street.

0.1 Turn left onto Mamane Street (Route 240).

8.7 Turn around at Waipio Valley Lookout.

17.2 Turn right onto Puakalo Street.

17.3 Turn right onto Akia Street.

17.4 Turn left into Honokaa Park.

Mamane Street has both smooth pavement and comfortable shoulders almost the entire way to the lookout. This area does not experience much local traffic, but at times it gets crowded with tour buses and visitors in rental cars.

At the lookout, you will see why so many people come here. Waipio Valley is a spectacular chasm that is cut 1,000 feet deep. From the viewpoint, you can look down into the valley, where rows of white, foamy waves wash up on a stark, black-sand beach. The valley has a flat floor, and the land is used to cultivate a number of crops, including kalo (taro).

The steep valley walls are lush and green and are cut by numerous waterfalls. This water irrigates the wetland taro crops before emptying into a stream that flows to the sea. You might see people fishing from the ocean shore or from boats in the deep waters outside Waipio Bay.

You can take a shuttle tour from the lookout down to the valley below, via a steep access road that requires a four-wheel-drive vehicle. Mountain bikers will have no problem riding down, but the climb back up will challenge even the most fit rider. You can also walk to the bottom.

For a thousand years Hawaiians have lived in this valley and used it just as it's being used today. In ancient Hawaii the valley was famous for its pigs and its abundance of food. Even today as you walk the trails in the valley, you will find breadfruit, mountain apples, coconuts, bananas, lilikoi (passion fruit), avocados, and guavas.

So why don't more people live here? First of all, the valley does not have the services of a modern subdivision. And you will see that the valley floor is just above sea level, with no barriers to protect it from the sea. In 1946 a tsunami devastated the valley, destroying homes and washing out crops. In 1979 a flood ripped through the valley, causing similar destruction.

The ride back to Honokaa from the valley lookout is slightly uphill, and you might find the trade winds working against you. Steady pedaling pays off, however, and soon you will be back in Honokaa.

About the Author

William L. Walters is a native of Hawaii and a graduate of the University of Hawaii with a degree in journalism. He has spent the past sixteen years bicycling through the Hawaiian island chain and every week clocks about 200 bicycling miles. He has provided race coverage and served as a contributing editor of *Pacific Velo News* and has written cycling and hiking itineraries for local organizations. His seven awards as a competitive cyclist include first place in the 1995 Waimanalo Road Race.